O9-AIE-436

How to Retire in Paradise for $19 a Day

prepared by the Editors of

International Living

How to Retire in Paradise for $19 a Day
Second edition
First published 2005

Copyright © 2006 by Agora Ireland Publishing & Services Ltd.

Agora Ireland Publishing & Services Ltd.
5 Catherine Street
Waterford
Ireland

Compiled by Emily Furlong

Copy-editor: Marsha Lisak

Assistant Editor: Donna Garvin

Graphic Design: Shannon Roberts

ISBN 978-1-905720-02-6

No part of this publication may be reproduced or transmitted in any form
or by any means, electronic or mechanical, including photocopying and
recording or by any information storage or retrieval system without the
written permission of the publisher.

While every effort has been made to provide accurate, up-to-date information, the authors and publisher accept no responsibility for loss, injury, or
inconvenience sustained by any person using this book. 120B000826

Table of Contents

Introduction

Imagine lounging on your deck, a cocktail in hand, the quiet turquoise waters of the Caribbean spread out before you...

Or picture yourself relaxing in a flower-filled courtyard where lavender bougainvillea tumbles over stucco walls, while the sweet perfume of frangipani fills the air at dusk.

Maybe you dream, instead, of a mountain retreat where the air is crisp and you live amidst expansive, snow-capped peaks.

Or perhaps it's an elegant pied-à-terre you envision...an apartment with 20-foot ceilings and crown molding, where geraniums fill your window boxes, and your days and evenings are busy with the cosmopolitan pleasures of big-city living...

Whatever you imagine, here's a guarantee: In the world's best havens, the dream can be yours—and for less than you can possibly imagine.

Whether your retirement is fast approaching or just something you often yourself find dreaming about, you've probably imagined spending it in some far-flung tropical haven. But moving to a country that you know very little about is a lot of hassle, right? It's probably not worth the time and effort to leave home, you think. Besides, all your family and friends are here.

Take it from us: it's worth it. If you look beyond your own shores you'll find that many countries around the world offer far greater benefits and advantages for retirees than those offered at home.

Indeed, your quality of life in your new home will exceed all of your dreams, the cost of living will be much lower...allowing you to do more of the passion-pursuing and less of the penny-pinching you're used to. And chances are you'll see your family and friends more often than ever, since you'll be living somewhere they'll want to visit—as a matter of fact, they'll probably come to be almost as passionate about your new home as you are!

A question of your priorities

According to the 2005 Mercer Human Resource Cost of Living study, it costs, on average, $2,483.64 per month to rent a two-bedroom apartment in New York. That means you'll pay $82 a day on rent alone! Want to retire in London? You'll pay even more. But, think about this: you can retire in beautiful, Udon Thani, Thailand or Vilcabamba, Ecuador for only $19 or less per day—and that includes not only rent but food, utilities, health care, dining out regularly and, in Thailand, even maid service.

People often miscalculate what they will spend day-to-day when they hit retirement. Granted, you won't have to pay for dry cleaning your work suits...gas will be cheaper to run when you're not sitting in traffic for hours on end...and you may save on parking. But in other areas of your life you'll find you'll be spending a lot more. What will you do with all your extra time? Golf? Skydive? Take art classes? Go to language school? All good ideas, but it will cost you...if you stay home. Why not live on a golf course, learn a language first-hand, live near Mayan ruins, for a lot less money?

One of the simplest ways to improve your retirement lifestyle is to choose the retirement destination offering you more of what you want, at the best price. It's a question of priorities. What's important to you?

Is cost of living Number One on your priority list? If so, you can rent a nice three-bedroom house in Udon Thani in northern Thailand for $245 a month. Here, a part-time maid costs $50 a month, and you can eat out with the locals in the street kitchens and noodle shops, which serve delectable meals for 50 to 60 cents. On Udon Thani's nine-hole golf course, prices for a round range from $3.12 to $5.20.

Is health care what you care about most? In Honduras, where many physicians are U.S.-trained, a visit to the doctor costs between $5 and $15, with a private hospital room costing around $30 to $40 a day. Complex surgery can be performed for as little as $1,000 and minor surgeries for much less. Plus pharmaceutical drugs cost about half what they do in the U.S.

Maybe for you weather is the key consideration. They don't call Ecuador "The Land of Eternal Sunshine" for nothing. Lying directly on the equator, the entire country enjoys 12 hours of direct equatorial sunlight 365 days a year. But because of its varied topography, just about any type of weather, except arctic tundra, can be found here. So whether you want sun, sun, sun, or cool afternoons stretching into cooler evenings, you will be comfortable in this climate.

Are your must-haves telecommunications and infrastructure? In Panama, you can get to the airport quickly and efficiently. Thanks to a long-time U.S. presence dating back to its interests in the canal, Panama's infrastructure is first-world. Not only are the roads free of potholes, high-speed Internet is the norm, rather than the exception. Your international phone calls go through the first time, every time. If efficiency and reliability are important to you, give Panama a closer look.

Or is it safety what you care about most? Believe it or not, Panama is the safest place in Central or South America. Panamanians are extremely friendly and welcome foreign tourists and residents with open arms. There isn't the envy or racial tension you might find in other economically deprived areas where westerners have swept in. Moreover, the family circle is important here—much more so than in the States or much of Europe—as is religion. This all makes for a very safe and comfortable environment.

How about having accessibility to the U.S.? At no other time have the benefits of living in Mexico been more apparent—and easier to take advantage of. Not just for U.S. citizens, but for Canadians, Europeans, South Americans...anyone looking for great weather, low prices, and rich culture.

Friendly people? If socializing and friendship are high on your list, consider Italy. As the Italian writer Luigi Barzini has said, "Italy made and still makes unwanted people feel wanted, unimportant people feel important." This country is very forgiving toward foreigners. For example, you can make a complete pig's ear of the language and nobody will sneer or get impatient with you.

Maybe you aren't anywhere close to retirement. Nevertheless, it's important to think about and plan for your future. Like every phase in your life, you'll be surprised how fast retirement creeps up on you.

Secure your dream location for when you do retire. The most desirable places in the world are being snapped up as people like you begin to realize the potential they offer. Find what you are looking for, do your research. The time to stake a claim to your dream retirement home— your own beachfront, lakeside, or mountaintop retreat—might very well be right now, while it's still priced within your reach.

Panama

Where in the world can you retire at 19 years of age?

Good question. And the answer is, only one place in the world: Panama.

Every year, *International Living* publishes our Global Retirement Index based on our global search for the best places to live, work, invest, and retire. In 2005, for the fifth year running, Panama takes first place, hands down. Panama's rating is no surprise to us; our last five reports have shown that no other country on earth has such a generous program to attract pensioners and retirees. But even we were shocked to find that in Panama it's possible to qualify for the *pensionado* retirement) program at the tender age of 19.

A new way of looking at retirement!

Panama is a forward-looking country. They realize that "retirement" is being redefined in the 21st century, and that the new generation of retirees has little in common with retirees of 50 years ago. In Panama, retirement isn't based on age: it's based on income. For example, if you have a pension or benefit program that pays you a minimum of $500 per month, you qualify as a retiree. The only other requirement is that you are at least 19 years old.

By meeting such basic requirements as having a modest income and no criminal record, you will qualify for a generous package of retiree benefits and discounts, including 50% off hotel reservations, 30% off public transport, 20% off doctor visits—and much more.

Just as important, Panama is safe, stable, and friendly. And it boasts the best health care and infrastructure in Central America! But these are only the bold headlines. As you take time to learn more about Panama, you'll find it keeps looking better and better. Its climate is unrivalled in the world, with topical rain forests, temperate mountains, and warm, tropical white sand beaches. Its wildlife is abundant, with most of the bird species in North America, and its pristine natural setting is an eco-tourist's dream. No wonder that the Smithsonian's Tropical Research Center is located in Barrio Colorado. Plus, unlike its neighbors, Panama is a stranger to hurricanes!

Bocas del Toro, the most popular but still little-known tourist destination, attracts those in search of adventures off the beaten trail, in a relaxed Caribbean setting, and everything you could desire in a tropical paradise: You can snorkel in clear, warm water, fish, sail, you name it. Or you can explore the territories of the seven indigenous peoples of Panama found in remote locations around the country. In Bocas, for example, you'll discover the Ngoebe-Buglé villages, where Indians live just as they have for centuries.

Panama is a safe country offering first-world benefits

First, let's start with some perspective on Panama. Panama is a safe, stable nation. There are no U.S. army bases—the Panama Canal was given back to the Panamanian government in 1999—but the longtime U.S. presence left in its wake the benefit of a modern infrastructure. Today, Panama is more like a First-World country than a developing nation. In Panama, things work. You can make an inter-national phone call (at very reasonable rates) anytime of day—and calls go through. You can e-mail over reliable, high-speed Internet connections. The roads are convenient, paved, and pothole-free.

Panama City certainly is the most affordable cosmopolitan city in this hemisphere. Which explains why *International Living* rates Panama as its top choice in the world for inexpensive, First-World city living. Many visitors are surprised at the Panama City skyline, where skyscrapers tower, and bright lights invitingly line the harbor.

In Panama you'll find any type of cuisine you might have an appetite for, along with shopping malls, dry cleaners, pizza delivery, first-run movies, top-notch hotels—in short, every imaginable necessity, amenity, and luxury imaginable. On some city blocks, where modern city-life abounds, you'll have to remind yourself you are in Central America—and, best yet, these luxuries and services are a fraction of the price you would expect to pay.

In addition to city life, Panama offers affordable living on the Pacific coast, (and on the tropical island of Contadora), plus one of the world's best mountain escapes in the inland Chiriqui region of Boquete.

Panama's very low cost of living

Monthly expenses in Panama are extremely reasonable. You may expect to pay:

- Apartment rental: $400 (unfurnished); $550 (furnished)

- Utilities (including electricity, cable TV, landline): $135

- Food/household goods: $200

- Maid service (part-time): $75

- Dining out (twice weekly): $40

- Transportation: car, $80 for gas, and $650 yearly car insurance (you can get around the city in a taxi for about $1 per way)

Total monthly costs (including furnished apartment, and running a car) is only about $1,134—that's $37 a day to live well in a first-world city!

One more thing: Panama is one of the best places in the hemisphere for a private offshore bank account, a multinational corporation, or a new business.

A safe stable government—with investment incentives

Around 10 years ago, when *International Living* first started researching Panama, we expected to find a rough and unstable government. We expected shabby conditions, and general squalor. We expected anti-American sentiment. Instead, as you can see, we found the exact opposite. We believe that Panama is the safest, most stable place in Central America.

Five years ago, after becoming so convinced of Panama's promise, *International Living* set up a local office in the historical city of Casco

Viejo, just 30 minutes by taxi from Panama City on the pacific coast. Here, our team is in residence provide our readers with first-hand information about living and retiring in Panama, either part- or full-time. Our staff mambers in Panama have made a new life in this amazing part of the world, and they would love to help you do the same.

And we're not the only ones who love it here…for the past eight years, the Panamanian government has focused on attracting foreigners to help build the country's economy. Believing that foreign investment will help the country as a whole, it has passed more than 40 laws protecting foreign investment rights, including the Investments Stability Law, guaranteeing equal rights for foreign and national investors.

Major companies in Panama include Federal Express, DHL, Price Costco, Bell South, Kansas City Southern Railways, ICA Construction), Cable & Wireless, Evergreen, Warranty Company of the Americas, and Hutchinson Whampoa. Continental Airlines (and Copa Airlines), and American Airlines have hubs here, plus you'll find just about every American franchise you can imagine on the streets of Panama City.

Additionally—and very conveniently—Panama uses the U.S. dollar as its legal tender, which insulates its economy from global shocks. During the Asian monetary crisis of 1998, for instance, Panama became one of the healthiest economies in Latin America.

The world's best *Pensionado* Program

For the last 15 years or so, adventurous Americans flocked to Costa Rica to retire. Some do still. But many more are reconsidering once they realize Costa Rica is no longer the pensioner's paradise it once was. Prices are high, bureaucracy is stifling, taxes are burdensome, and its famed *pensionado* program is now defunct.

Panama is now positioning itself as the "New Costa Rica." Like that country, Panama boasts rich cultural and natural attractions, and has put together the most appealing retirement program of special benefits that you'll find anywhere in the world today.

You may be thinking, "Pensioner? Retiree? That leaves me out." If so, think again. The rules for becoming a pensioner and qualifying for this visa program in Panama are not what you think.

In fact, anyone over the age of 18 may apply and qualify as a *pensionado* in Panama, provided he or she can show evidence of a guaranteed pension income of $500 per month ($600 per month per couple). To qualify, all you need is a pension from a gove rnment agency (e.g., social security, disability, armed forces), or from a company.

As a *pensionado* in Panama, you will be entitled to:

- 50% off entertainment—such as movies, theaters, concerts, and sporting events—anywhere in the country

- 30% off bus, boat, and train fares

- 25% off airline tickets

- 50% off hotel stays, Monday–Thursday

- 30% off hotel stays, Friday–Sunday

- 25% off restaurants

- 15% off fast-food restaurants

- 15% off hospital bills (if no insurance applies)

- 10% off prescription medicine

- 20% off medical consultations

- 15% off dental and eye exams

- 20% off professional and technical services

- 50% off closing costs for home loans...and the list goes on.

In addition, you are entitled to a one-time exemption from duties on the importation of household goods (up to $10,000) and an exemption every two years from duties for the importation or local purchase of a car.

Moreover, Panama's *pensionado* law stipulates that anyone entering the country today as a qualified pensioner, is guaranteed pensioner status as long as he or she chooses to stay in the country. This is an important point: By law, should the requirements for a retirement visa change at a later date, the new requirements will not affect a person's existing *pensionado* status (assuming the pensioner maintains the required minimum level of income).

When the Costa Rican government did away with its *pensionado* laws, and failed to protect its existing pensioners, many American pensioners suddenly lost their status. Not having such a law ended Costa Rica's position as a top retirement haven.

Panama took a lesson from Costa Rica, and designed its *pensionado* law so that today's pensioners will be protected tomorrow.

Panama offers one of the easiest and most affordable residency programs in the world...

The cost of completing Panama's entire residency program will come to no more than a few thousand dollars. Compare that number to residency, and passport programs elsewhere in the world, where legal costs alone can amount to more than $10,000—and that's not even factoring in the capital required to qualify. In comparison to Panama, other programs in the Caribbean require spending up to—and beyond—a quarter of a million dollars. For instance, the Cayman Islands and the Bahamas require large financial commitments in local property. And a passport to Dominica, St. Kitts, and Nevis can cost upward of $250,000.

The visa process for a residency (or *pensionado*) program in Panama is very simple. It's requires a one-time application with no renewals or additional fees. Your permit takes only a month or two to process. It's fast. It's affordable. It's easy. Unlike other residency programs requiring yearly renewal, the simplicity of Panama's program relieves you of hassle, and additional fees. In Panama, apply today and you'll have residency for life—and for no more than a few thousand dollars.

Panama is truly one of the best—if not *the* best—residency deals in the world today.

For the price, the benefits are incomparable. And it is an extraordinary opportunity—especially now. At *International Living*, we expect property prices to continue their rapid climb in Panama, just as prices rose in Costa Rica when they introduced their famed *pensionado* program. Now is the time to get in on the ground floor of what we believe to be the number one retirement haven in existence.

Of course, the Panama *pensionado* program will not net you a passport, but it will grant you residency rights for life. If you want, or need, a Panamanian passport for tax or other reasons, there are many other programs that can qualify you. For instance, you can start your own business with as little as a $40,000 investment, and, within nine years, you'll be granted a Panamanian passport. This is just one of the many ways in which you can qualify to live, retire, or do business in Panama.

Explanation of Panama's most popular visas

As a benefit to our readers, we recommend attorney Rainelda Mata-Kelly who represents both Panamanian and foreign clients with Panama's residency and *pensionado* programs. Rainelda, who holds a Master's of Law from Cornell University, founded the London office of a Panamanian law firm in 1983. In 1991, she became a Miami correspondent for *La Prensa*, a Panamanian newspaper, and went on to be that paper's executive editor. Since 1989, she has been engaged in her own practice, specializing in commercial and shipping law.

Rainelda created the following description to explain the requirements and features of the most popular programs currently available for people wishing to retire to Panama.

The Tourist Pensioner Visa (*Turista Pensionado*)

This visa is granted indefinitely and is designed for persons whose pension (from a government entity or private corporation) is $500 or more per month ($600 or more for a couple per month). The benefits of the tourist pensioner visa include a one-time exemption of duties for the importation of household goods (up to $10,000) and an exemption every two years of import duties for a car. You will still need to pay sales tax; however, please note that under this visa you will not qualify to acquire Panamanian nationality.

Application for this visa requires:

- Valid passport (with at least one year remaining before expiration);

- Nine passport-size photos (gentlemen in suits and ties; ladies in blouses/dresses with sleeves);

- Original letter or certification, signed by your pension provider, as evidence of pensioner status. The letter should state entitlement to a pension of more than $500 (as well as $100 per month for each dependent you will be bringing under your visa), and should be duly authenticated;

- Good Standing certificate, issued by the Registrar of Companies and duly authenticated, if the pension is granted by a private corporation. Please also bring a bank statement showing pension deposits;

- Police record from your place of residence for the past five years, duly authenticated; and

- Marriage certificate (if your spouse is to be included as a dependent on your visa), duly authenticated.

Private Income Retiree Visa (*Rentista Retirado*)

The private income visa for retirees is designed for persons who don't have a monthly pension, are no longer working, and have received a retirement lump sum. As a visa requirement, the retirement sum is to be deposited on a five-year Certificate of Deposit (CD) with the National Bank of Panama, and must yield at least $750 per month. As such, the face value of the certificate of deposit, at current rates, would need to be approximately $225,000. The visa is renewable every five years, so long as the CD is renewed.

The Private Income Retiree Visa includes such benefits as a traveling Panamanian passport (that does not grant nationality), a one-time exemption from duties for the importation of new household goods (up to $10,000), and an exemption every two years from import duties for a car. You will still need to pay sales tax.

The following requirements must be met to apply for this visa:

* Valid passport (with at least one year remaining before expiration);

* Nine passport-size photos (gentlemen in suit and tie; ladies in blouses or dresses with sleeves);

* Police record from your place(s) of residence for the past five years, duly authenticated;

* Marriage certificate (if your spouse is to be included as dependent in your visa), duly authenticated; and

* Adequate funds to establish a certificate of deposit with the National Bank of Panama for five years, for a monthly yield of $750.

Person of Means Visa (*Solvencia Económica Propia*)

Designed for financially independent individuals, the pension of means visa can be obtained by those who wish to live in Panama without a desire to work or start a business.

To qualify for this visa, a person must have ONE of the following:

A. Two-year certificate of deposit in any local bank with a minimum balance of $200,000. After these two years, the funds may be withdrawn; or

B. Investment in real estate in the Republic of Panama in the amount of at least $200,000, and present proof of other means of income; or

C. Two-year certificate of deposit in any local bank with a minimum balance of $120,000 and investment in real estate in the Republic of Panama in the amount of at least $80,000, as well as proof of other means of income to support his/her stay in Panama.

Both the certificate of deposit and the real estate mentioned above must be in the personal name of the applicant (i.e., not under a corporation). For each dependent, the applicant must show an additional $75 monthly income.

The following requirements are needed to apply for the person of means visa:

- Valid passport (with at least one year remaining before expiration);

- Nine passport-size photos (gentlemen in suit and tie; ladies in blouses or dresses with sleeves);

- Police record from your place of residence for the past five years, duly authenticated;

- Marriage certificate (if your spouse is to be included as dependent in your visa), duly authenticated; and

- Required funds to open the Certificate of Deposit, or invest in real estate.

This visa is granted provisionally for one year and, after renewal, is granted permanently with the right to be issued a *cedula* (identity card). Five years after obtaining the permanent visa, holders will be eligible to apply for Panamanian nationality.

A word of advice on obtaining a visa

Bear in mind that if you wish to conduct business during your stay in Panama (visits to the Immigration Department, appointments to open bank accounts, etc.) you should wear rather conservative clothing. Shorts, sandals, tank tops, and other such items of casual clothing are generally frowned upon. Moreover, government offices will bar entrance to anyone who's dressed in such attire. The visa information above should not be deemed legal advice, but rather as a brief overview of some of the visas available in Panama. It applies solely to nationals of Canada, the U.S., and most of the European Union. An evaluation of your individual case may be necessary to determine the visa best suited to your circumstances.

- ***Rainelda Mata-Kelly, LL.M.**, *Law Offices, Suite #305-307, Balboa Plaza, Balboa Avenue (building address); P.O. Box 0818-00534, Panama City, Panama (mailing address); tel. (507)263-4305; fax (507)264-2868; e-mail: rmk@matakelly.com; website www.mata-kelly.com.*

Rainelda is our recommended attorney in Panama. If you wish to find out more information about Panama's many attractive visa programs, please contact her.

Living in Panama

Contadora—A Pacific paradise

If you're in search of sand and sun, Panama has tropical beauty in abundance on both the Caribbean and Pacific coasts. On the Pacific Ocean side of the country, *International Living* recommends the island of Contadora, the seventh biggest of the 90 named islands in the Pearl Islands archipelago, in the Bay of Panama, just off the coast of Panama City. We're so impressed by the Pearl Islands and, specifically, the absolute privacy offered by the island of Contadora, that we've invested here ourselves But don't just take our word for it, here's what friend and contributing editor to *IL* Bob Fordi has to say about Contadora:

This is the stuff of travel magazine cover photos: turquoise waters, 13 white-sand beaches, secluded coves, bright red and yellow fishing boats, swaying palm and cashew trees, giant coral reefs, coconuts, mangoes, parrots, hummingbirds, pelicans, sea turtles, and bright tropical flowers. I even saw gray and orca whales just off the island's shores.

Today Contadora Island is a closely guarded secret playground for wealthy and famous political leaders, writers, entertainers, and businessmen—not only from Panama, but from all over the world.

This island is well off most tourists' radar screens, which is exactly what the people who come to Contadora love about it. It has only two resorts, one small condo complex, three small B&Bs, a few small homes, and several dozen large mansions. It's a 650-acre island. During peak times, the population swells to about 1,500.

During most of the year, you'll rarely find more than 500 people on Contadora. That's not to say the island is lacking in amenities. It has a small airstrip and daily, 15-minute, round-trip flights to and from Panama City cost about $64. Or you can take the ferry, which runs

---

*In the interest of full disclosure, *International Living* receives commissions from referrals to Rainelda Mata-Kelly.

every weekend. There's a new medical center on the island, several decent restaurants, a small 9-hole golf course, a few small shops, a scooter rental shop, and a well-stocked grocery store. Beach-front living is still possible here, and on beaches as beautiful and private as you can desire.

Plus, Contadora is safe. Residents say they feel comfortable walking anywhere on the island, anytime, even in the middle of the night. At time of going to print, prices range from $147,500 for a one-bedroom villa to $245,000 for a three-bed. And these prices on a small island graced with white sand beaches, crystal clear, warm water and tropical flora and fauna.

For more information contact Bob Fordi. He is the agent for the Villas at Contadora. Bob can be reached by *e-mail: rfordi@worldnet.att.net; tel./fax (240)465-0523; website: www.contadora villas.com.**

Boquete—Mountain paradise

Balmy is nice, but the forested mountains of Boquete offer another kind of paradise in Panama. This little valley, located in the mountainous Chiriqui region at an elevation of 3,500 feet, is one of the world's most wondrous refuges. Due to its elevation, daytime temperatures rarely dip below 70° F in Boquete and rarely climb above 80° F. Nights are cool and comfortable. Boquete is ideal, therefore, as either a year-round, full-time retreat...or as a place to escape to for several weeks of the year. In our minds, it's hard to imagine a better haven than this little village.

Boquete's lush green hills, flowing rivers, and spectacular waterfalls make it one of the most unspoiled retirement retreats in the world today. Although banana, mango, and palm trees abound, this is coffee country and during the harvest season, the local Indians come down from the hills to work in the fields. The men call and sing to each other as they pick. Their children run through the fields and play in the streams. This is Boquete—where spring reigns eternal.

*In the interest of full disclosure International Living receives commissions from referred sales at Contadora.

Boquete is located at the base of the tallest peak in Panama, the extinct volcano of Baru. The surrounding mountains are blanketed with coffee, banana, mango, and palm trees. The Caldera River rushes through the middle of town and out to the Pacific Ocean, less than 30 miles away. From the upper rim of the valley you can see the ocean, and the border of Costa Rica in the distance, as well as the storybook village below.

Boquete began as a small farming community that prospered due to its rich volcanic soil, and temperate climate. Development, however, has been slow. While the nearby city of David has grown into an agricultural and industrial center in the Province of Chiriqui, Boquete has remained a quiet and peaceful place, much as it has been for centuries.

Because of the superb climate, the area around Boquete is lush and verdant—Panamanians call it the "Valley of Flowers and Eternal Spring." It offers all manner of outdoor activities such as hiking, biking, bird watching, horse-riding, whitewater rafting, trout fishing, and gardening. The town is renowned throughout Panama for its coffee and its flowers. The Boquete Flower and Coffee Fair attracts thousands of visitors from all over the world every January.

Coffee beans are picked from October through February in Boquete, primarily by the Guaymi Indians. The harvest season is a festive time when families, in traditional dress, come down from the mountains to work. The conditions in Boquete are, in fact, ideal for growing coffee, which is shipped to Europe and North America.

We're not the only ones taking note of what's going on in Boquete, which has been ranked a number-one retirement destination in the Western Hemisphere. According to the May/June 2001 issue of AARP's *Modern Maturity* (one of the largest consumer magazines in the world, with more than 20 million readers) Boquete rated the fourth-best retirement destination in the world, following such developed locations as Costa del Sol, Spain; Cinque Terre, Italy, and Provence, France. Since 2001, retirees have flocked to this retirement gem. With banks, B&Bs, hotels, and museums, Boquete is fast becoming an eco-tourist's mecca.

Nine facts you may not know about Panama

1. The U.S. dollar is the official currency.
2. Most people are bilingual in Spanish and English.
3. Panama's emphasis in education has resulted in a 90.8% literacy rate.
4. Panamanians enjoy the highest per capita incomes in Central America.
5. Panama's water supply is safe to drink in most areas, without fear of "Montezuma's revenge."*
6. Medical care is abundant, inexpensive, and of high quality (doctors don't have to pay the high malpractice insurance fees they do in the U.S.).
7. The infrastructure rivals that of the U.S. with accessible roads, international airports with daily flights to the U.S., and public and mass transportation.
8. Panama's constitution guarantees religious freedom.
9. Considered the banking capital of Central America, Panama is a privacy and tax haven second only to Switzerland.

From our vantage point in Panama, we've noticed that Boquete has more to offer every time we look. In the last few years a number of new developments have sprung up, including a riverside restaurant, a hotel, a folklore shop with arts and crafts from Central America, a visitors' center, and a sports center with basketball courts and baseball fields. Numerous Mexican, Chinese, Italian, and American restaurants are new to the area. This rural community now has access to web designers, antiques shops, dentists, attorneys, accountants—even a video shop that offers DVD and video rentals. Boquete even has an English-language online e-zine, the *Boquete Times*, which chronicles the arts and cultural events in and around Boquete. The site offers a full directory of local businesses and services. (Check them out at *www.theboquetetimes.com*.)

Boquete even boasts a free English/Spanish newspaper called *Bajareque Times* that launched in 2005.

This quaint, rural little place is blossoming, and becoming remarkably cosmopolitan.

---

* Montezuma's revenge is an unpleasant dose of traveler's diarrhea in Latin America. Also referred to as the "Gringo Gallop", and the "Aztec Two-step" by locals.

What things cost in Boquete

With all these advantages and conveniences you might expect things to be expensive in Boquete—but they aren't.

Here are a few examples of the costs of local goods and services in Boquete:

- A home can be built for about $50 to $60 per square foot.

- Finished 2,500-square-foot, older homes cost $80,000 to $150,000.

- Smaller lots near the town of Boquete are between $100,000 and $250,000 (quarter to half acre).

- Unskilled labor costs $6.40 per day.

- A full-time, live-in maid costs $120 a month.

- A beer at a bar costs 35 cents; a cup of coffee, 30 cents.

- A haircut and shave can cost as little as $2 each.

- An afternoon at a beauty salon is $8.

- Electricity is about 12 cents per kilowatt-hour…and, remember, you don't need air conditioning in Boquete.

- Water bills are $18 per year.

- Telephone service costs roughly $30 per month.

- Internet access is $14 per month; wireless is available for a bit more.

- Cellular telephone service costs approximately $30 per month, plus a per-minute charge of around 22 cents.

- Direct TV will cost you approximately $30 per month.

Rent a home in Boquete for $500 a month

Although prices have risen along with popularity, you can still rent a home in Boquete at an excellent rate. We found several homes renting for around $500 a month—small, but clean, and functional.

(Contact *International Living* Panama for details.) You can spend more, of course. One three-bedroom, two-bathroom home in town, very nicely furnished, rents for $1,100 a month.

Hotel accommodation in Boquete

- **Los Establos**, *tel. (507)720-2685; e-mail: losestablos@cometoboquete.com; website: www.valleescondido.biz/losestablos.* This is the nicest hotel in Boquete. Price: as low as $90 per night.

- **Hotel Panamonte**, *tel. (507)720-1327; fax (507)720-2211; e-mail: montana@chiriqui.com.* This is a charming little place, with good food. Be sure to take home some of their strawberry jam. Price: $66 per night.

- **Los Quetzales Cabins & Hotels**, *Volcan Baru National Park, Chiriqui Province; tel. (507)771-2182; fax (507)771-2226.* Price: $60 per night.

- **Isla Verde Hotel**, *tel. (507)720-2533, fax (507)720-2751, cell (507)677-4009; e-mail: islaverde@cwpanama.net.* Here you can stay in a Roundhouse, which has its own kitchen area. It also has two apartments that face a beautiful river with spectacular views. Have breakfast in the colorful garden. Please keep in mind that there is no restaurant in this hotel, but you are a five-minutes' walk from a town. You can stay here for $50 per couple.

Living in the Panama highlands...David

If you're looking for a place to retire, in our view it simply doesn't get any better than the highland areas of Panama, especially when it comes to value combined with convenience. A 30-minute drive from Boquete, on a perfectly paved and modern road, brings you to the city of David (pronounced "Da-VEED"). Here you'll find everything, including two U.S.-style grocery stores, a Price Smart, two private hospitals, and six new-car dealerships.

A small airport serves David with daily flights to Panama City and Bocas Del Toro on the Caribbean coast. You can fly to these destinations for $25 to $50 each way. A 30-minute drive on a four-lane road will take you to the Costa Rican border. Also available is a first-class Mercedes bus to Panama City for $15 (movies included!). The road from David to Panama City is now a mostly four-lane highway that can be driven in about five hours. This coastal drive is dotted with beautiful beaches along the way.

One kilometer from the David airport is a marina accepting large yachts to small boats. The fishing and diving just off the coast are superb. A two-hour drive on a fine road takes you to the Caribbean Coast and Bocas Del Toro (literally translated: "the mouth of the bull").

The Gamboa Rainforest Resort— luxury living in a natural setting

The Gamboa Rainforest Resort is a luxury five-star destination, located on 340 acres in the heart of the Soberania National Park. It's just a 30-minute drive from Panama City, but its location will make you feel as if you're hours from civilization, yet offers the highest luxuries. The hotel and conference center has 107 rooms, several restaurants and bars, a full-service spa, tennis courts, and an incredible pool. Panama's newest golf course is only 10 minutes away.

However, despite these modern amenities, nature reigns supreme. Amazingly, these resort facilities are perfectly integrated into the natural landscape with great respect to the surrounding rainforest and the nearby Indian reservation.

This resort is a nature lover's dream. There's hiking, birdwatching, kayaking, and world-class fishing, all just a stroll away. In fact, the resort maintains Panama's only butterfly farm, where you can literally witness the life cycle of some of the country's most beautiful butter-flies. There's also a serpentarium, an orchid farm, and a full-service marina. From the marina you can take a kayak, a boat—even a pedal boat—down jungle rivers. Along the way you might spot one of the famed howler monkeys, an otter, or an alligator.

We recommend the five-star Gamboa Rainforest Resort for its splendid comfort and outstanding natural setting. Partake in any number of ecological tours, have a gourmet meal, or ride the only rainforest canopy tram in Panama. You can get a one-bedroom, historic villa apartment for $120 per night, not including the 10% tax. (*International Living* readers can visit the resort at discounted rates. If you think you'd enjoy a stay in the rainforest, drop us a line at our offices in Panama City, and we'll organize a discount for you.)

Three *IL* readers relocated to Panama and haven't looked back

by Thom Hickling
Panama uses the U.S. dollar

Everyone else is advising retirees to relocate in Costa Rica, but *International Living* (*IL*) readers were onto that news 20 years ago! Now homes there are selling for 10 times the price our readers paid back then.

This is a story of three couples who have pulled up stakes and relocated to Panama—each with a different story to tell. All, however, were attracted to this country by the low property prices and affordable cost of living, as well as the many retirement incentives they're able to take advantage of. Read on and be inspired...

Piece of Paradise in Panama

Bill and Carole Keene sold their house in Maryland, and will head to Panama next month to reclaim their already-shipped household goods and automobile. Their hearts were captured by a four-bedroom mountain chalet with nearly an acre of beautifully landscaped grounds, and views of valleys and mountains. But for them the *pièce de resistance* of their new home was the Pacific Ocean view.

"We are not rich people," says Bill Keene, "and an early retirement for us means a limited fixed income, and savings that need to be stretched over many years to come. A low-cost locale like Panama is the ideal place for us to spend our later years in comfort and tranquillity, and yet still be just 75 minutes away from a major city with First-World amenities. We have it all: great health care, jazz clubs, casinos, modern malls, and direct air connections to several major U.S. cities." He added: "The good weather, a dollar-based economy, and friendly people are a bonus."

"After reading *International Living*'s articles and reports, we settled on two possible locations—Belize and Panama. We ordered *IL*'s *Owner's Manuals* for those two countries, and they proved to be invaluable. So we contacted *IL*'s recommended real estate people, and arranged for a three-day tour to look at properties that met our criteria. We are in the process of relocating to Panama now. Not only were *IL*'s contacts helpful in our search, but they have become our new friends!"

Bill and Carole own a near-acre of paradise, and employ a gardener who maintains the landscaping and fruit trees at an affordable price for them, and a fair wage for him. In addition to the beautiful flowers—the bougainvillea are spectacular—and lush vegetation, they have banana, apple, cashew, mango, pepper, and papaya trees, plus, they were told, there are shrimp and crab in the brook that runs along their property line.

Their home sits on an east-facing, Pacific shoreline near Punta Chame. The spectacular ocean sunrises visible off the left side of their veranda, and the sun sets over the mountains from the front of their house, offering a unique effect.

Bill enthuses, "It's almost like a second sunrise, because the clouds in the eastern sky light up again at sunset in rose and pink pastels. I suppose that it's caused by the mountains shielding the lower part of eastern sky from the golden beams of the setting sun. We may never leave! We've fallen in love with this place, and with each other all over again."

The Keenes' decision to choose Panama also had the advantage of timing. Panama's real estate market is bouncing back from a slowdown brought about by the phased departure of tens of thousands of Americans, when the Canal was turned over to the Panamanian administration in 1999, and major U.S. military bases were closed. Moving such a large number of relatively high-income residents from a small economy created an incredible buyers market.

Bill continues: "We are family-centered people, and the only things we miss are the impromptu get-togethers with our three grown kids, our grandchildren, other family, and friends. We're compensating by budgeting for four trips home each year, and making plans for family and friends to visit us in our newfound paradise. The good news is that we know they'll want to visit such a wonderful place."

The baby boomers are on the move

Donna Hawley never really wanted to leave her home in Minneapolis, but her husband, Jim, always dreamed of moving to a warm, sunny overseas destination. He read about Panama in *International Living* and told Donna he was traveling there to look at property. She thought he was crazy.

But by the time he was about to leave, she decided to book a flight and join him. When these baby boomers returned to Minnesota, they were the owners of not one, but two homes in Panama: an apartment in a Panama City high-rise, and a residence in a golf community near the beach, about an hour and a half from the capital.

They closed their wholesale optical business and moved to Panama. Donna was quickly able to qualify for the generous Panamanian *pensionado* program. Anyone over the age of 18 can apply for the *pensionado* by having a guaranteed pension income of only $500 per month ($600 per month for a couple). It must be a pension from a government agency (e.g., social security, disability, armed forces, etc.) or from a company. For more information, contact Rainelda Mata-Kelly, *e-mail: rmk@mata-kelly.com.*

Even though Jim and Donna aren't retired—or rich—they now have a fantastic new life. To purchase *both* their panoramic bay-view apartment in the center of cosmopolitan Panama City, and their 2,000-square-foot townhouse on an 18-hole golf course, they spent about $340,000! Donna plays much more golf than she did in Minneapolis, now that she doesn't have to pay greens fees, and enjoys warm weather 12 months a year.

"It's a total adventure," Donna says. "I tell my friends to come on down, there's such a need for people with North American business experience. More Boomers and investors are coming, and people who know how to do business with Americans are in great demand here."

Jim quickly found a job managing a luxury resort on the Pearl Islands—Hacienda del Mar. The resort has 14 cabanas, each with breathtaking views to the beach, the sea, and the triple-canopy forest of the island. It's his dream job.

And Donna quickly found a job with Empresas Bern selling condos to Americans. "I love waking up looking at the water. I enjoy living here. It's like a small town. I'm so surprised how many friends I've made in such a short time." She adds, "I've heard how friendly Panamanians are from every person living here."

Friendly and stress-free Contadora

John and Cheryl Pasey are retirees from San Francisco who own a villa at Contadora Island, where they spend plenty of time each year. John tells us: "We thought we were buying a vacation home, but what we really got was a big new family of fellow island-dwellers," they say. "When someone catches fish, it turns into a social occasion with the other residents.

"Back in California, I'm allowed to keep only two fish, and sometimes I don't catch any. The fishing here is unbelievable! I catch something every time I go out. I was going to buy a boat but I don't really need to. I joined the marina, and someone is always ready to go fishing with me," he says.

John and Cheryl's enthusiasm for their new island life is palpable. Cheryl adds: "We can walk to the beach, and usually have it to ourselves. But when we see someone else they're always friendly. On this little island we're all friends."

To give you an idea of how gorgeous Contadora is, when the Shah of Iran was exiled he chose this island as his home. This exclusive location has been a secret destination of the super rich for decades. The crew from *Survivor* stayed here while shooting *Survivor: Pearl Islands*.

Even though the rich and famous live and visit here, Contadora isn't pretentious. John extols Contadora's virtues: "We were accepted here immediately. We feel like we fit right in."

The couple is also planning to buy a condo in the city since they've come to relish the cultural life of Panama's capital, Panama City. "Parts of the city feel like San Francisco, but with better weather," Cheryl says. "We stay at a great little hotel that costs $45 a night. When our daughter visits we get a suite for $60! We like it here so much we're going to buy a place of our own. That way we can have the peace and quiet of the island, along with the great restaurants and nightlife of the city."

Before retiring, John was an engineer with a waste-management business—work that took him to more than 50 countries. He knows the world. In 1999, he sold the business and retired.

Panama was John's destination of choice because he felt it offered the best options of any place in the world. This happy couple return to San Francisco often, but they now consider Panama their home.

"We're now able to rent our villa when we are away, which happened through word of mouth, and not by planning on our part," Cheryl admits. "Our friends simply wanted to enjoy the life we were telling them about. Now when we're not here, we rent our villa to them. Not long ago, we rented the place to some Italian tourists. They loved it and extended their stay. It's working out great for us."

- **Gamboa Rainforest Resort**, *Gamboa; tel. (507)314-9000; fax (507)314-9020; e-mail: reservations@gamboaresort.com; website: www.gamboaresort.com.*

Panama also offers the Summit Golf and Resort just 10 minutes away from the Gamboa Rainforest Resort. This world-class golf course and country club was originally opened in the 1940s for Americans working in the canal-zone. It is situated on a hill just outside the rainforest. The club offers an 18-hole Jeffrey Myers course, and a beautiful clubhouse with a dining room, bar, and swimming pool. Tennis and squash courts are under construction, and there are plans to build a small luxury hotel. Twenty-five-year memberships begin as low as $5,500, and the monthly dues are $135. Once a member, golf to your heart's content as there are no green fees for members. WorldGolf.com calls it the "best course in Central America" (even if they do list it under "South American" courses).

- **Summit Golf and Resort**, *tel. (507)232-4653; fax (507)232-4457; website: www.summitgolfpanama.com.*

Contacts

We've set up our team in Panama to help you. Please take advantage of their expertise. You'll find them in Casco Viejo, at the corner of Plaza Catedral, across from the Canal Museum. They're available weekdays 9 a.m. to 6 p.m., *tel. (507)212-0344; fax 507-212-3771; e-mail: Panama@InternationalLiving.com.*

Legal services

*   **Rainelda Mata-Kelly, LL.M.**, *Law Offices, Suite #305-307, Balboa Plaza, Balboa Avenue (building address); P.O. Box 9012, Panama 6, Panama (mailing address); tel. (507)263-4305; fax (507)264-2868; e-mail: rmk@mata-kelly.com; website www.mata-kelly.com.** Rainelda is our recommended attorney in Panama. If you wish to find out more information about Panama's many attractive visa programs, please contact her.

Medical emergencies

*   **Hospital Paitilla**, *Avenida Balboa 53; tel. (507)265-8800.*

*   **Farmacia Arrocha**, *Calle Aquilino de la Guardia (building address); tel.(507)223-4505.* This is a 24-hour pharmacy.

*   **Dr. Chang**, *Via Espana y via Porras (building address); tel. (507)223-9510 or (507)223-4590; mobile (507)626-3913.* If you need an emergency prescription, try Dr. Chang.

Panamanian government agencies

*   **Embassy of Panama (in the U.S.)**, *2862 McGill Terrace N.W., Washington, DC 20008; tel. (202)483-1407; fax (202)434-8413.*

*   **Panamanian Consulate (in the U.S.)**, *1212 Avenue of the Americas, 10th Floor, New York, N.Y. 10036; tel. (212)840-2450; fax (212)840-2469.*

*In the interest of full disclosure, *International Living* receives commissions from referrals to Rainelda Mata-Kelly.

Honduras

Doors carved with Mayan monkey gods lead into the master bedroom suite. Beautiful wooden furniture—a king-size bed, an eight-foot-tall mahogany wardrobe, a giant pigeonhole desk—stand out in contrast along the white walls. Marble steps take you into a giant, beautifully tiled shower room. The sound of waves fills the house as gentle ocean breezes waft through cotton curtains. A large picture window looks out to the Caribbean. All you can see for miles and miles is the white sand bay verging the blue-green sea, stretching towards the horizon.

Welcome to your retirement home in Honduras.

Honduras has all the makings of the perfect retirement haven: lush countryside with beaches and mountains, a tropical climate, a stable government, international airports, safe cities, friendly people, and, most importantly, a very low cost of living. You can eat well for just a few dollars a day in Honduras. The country produces rice, beans, plantains, bananas, mangos, pineapples, papayas, melons, oranges, and more, for pennies a kilo. Seafood is inexpensive and plentiful along the entire Caribbean coast.

The government will grant you retirement residency if you can prove, among other things, that you have at least $1,500 a month in third party, independent income. (If you prove you have put $50,000 into an approved project, you are exempt from the $1,500 monthly.) And, if you spend carefully, you can live comfortably on that $1,500. But keep in mind that living on the mainland will be quite a bit less expensive than living in the Bay Islands. As a rule, island living anywhere is more costly.

Wherever you live in Honduras, if you construct a house to take advantage of shady trees, cool breezes, and ceiling fans, and your wants are not extravagant, you can live easily on a very reasonable income. One couple we spoke with that lives on the Caribbean island Roatan, reports that they live comfortably, eat out a couple times a week, and spend about $1,000 a month. This cost seems to be the median price. At the other end of the spectrum, another Roatan resident with more extravagant tastes, told us that with her very large house, and air conditioning running all day, costs amount to about $3,000 a month.

In Honduras, retirement residency permits the importation of household goods, and your car, duty-free. Health care is extremely inexpensive. Prescription drugs, for example, cost one-tenth of what they cost in the U.S.

The day-to-day costs of living in Honduras are very low

Food is extremely inexpensive in Honduras. Shrimp boats bring in not only shrimp, but also crabs, lobsters, fish, and other seafood. You can buy lobster for less than $2 apiece. Or go out for dinner at the most expensive restaurants and order the lobster *con ajillo o parmesana* (garlic and cheese) for $20. (One of the best places on Roatan is Gio's, *in French Harbour; tel./fax (504)45-1536.*)

A good steak dinner at one of the finest restaurants in the country only costs about $7. You can drink Chilean wine for $1.70 a glass, $5 for a bottle. Four kinds of locally brewed beer—Nacional, Port Royal, Salva Vida, and Bahia—cost just 50 cents a bottle. A live-in maid, who will also shop and cook, costs only $40 to $60 a month. A couple can spend as little as $300 a month on groceries, including U.S. products, which are readily available. Fresh-baked coconut bread costs about 50 cents a loaf. (For the best bread on Roatan, head to the Midway Bakery, *tel. (504)45-1494*, managed by Alex Coleman. Their coconut bread is the specialty of the house.)

Rich Honduran coffee costs only $2 a pound. Fruits, rice, and vegetables can be had for less than 50 cents a kilo.

Utilities in Honduras are available and affordable. Electricity costs 24 cents a kilowatt hour, which means an electricity bill for as little as $20 a month if you live in a simple beach house. In a more luxurious home with all the extras—washing machine, clothes dryer, air-conditioning, a hot water heater, etc.—costs can range $60–$90 ($130 if you also want a television set and a stereo). Telephone costs have a base rate of $3 a month.

Garbage pickup costs $6 a month on Roatan, and a yardman costs about the same a day.

Special incentives for retirees in Honduras

Retirees are given special residency privileges not available to foreign investors or permanent residents. The retirement residency program in Honduras is similar to the *pensionado* program that Costa Rica offered for a short while in the 1980s. It takes as little as two months to establish retirement residency in Honduras. Once you have a residency visa, you can bring in household and personal goods—including your car—duty-free. Every five years, you may trade or sell your car and bring in another one, again duty-free.

Our favorite island retirement paradises—the Bay Islands

We recommend three areas in Honduras as the most desirable for retirement living; depending on your taste: Roatan, the most commercial, populated, and developed; Guanaja, the most pristine, with no roads or cars; and Utila, the most economical. All three belong to the beautiful Bay Islands.

Among the best-kept secrets in the Caribbean, these three locations are true tropical paradises. They are, however, far from cosmopolitan. You can't go out to the movies, for example, since there are no movie theaters, although Roatan now has several video stores, and several hotels show movies on Monday nights. There are a handful of restaurants, located in the few hotels on the island, with seafood, island specialties, and continental cuisine. And although you won't find attractions like golf courses, or many cultural attractions, you will find the archeologically-oriented Roatan Museum.

Honduras is perfect for those looking for the most beautiful beaches in all of Central America, with some of the best diving in the world, along with other like-minded retirees.

And if you get a hankering for a little action and want to make the jaunt to the city, you can fly to the mainland for just $30 round-trip.

For medical emergencies, there is access to a 24-hour medical transport plane, operated by Roatan Air Services, which flies to the mainland. (RAS cannot carry stretchers, so if a stretcher is needed, Atlantic Airlines will charter a plane).

Retirement "Eden" on the mainland—
low-cost living in a lush, Caribbean setting

Tela and Trujillo are our two favorite retirement havens located on the mainland of Honduras. These towns remain sleepers— virtually undiscovered gems boasting miles and miles of deserted Caribbean beaches.

Both Tela and Trujillo are those truly looking for a natural, unspoiled Edenic getaway. Far from being cosmopolitan, or even very developed, these areas do have a few restaurants serving fresh seafood dishes, rice, fruit, vegetables, and (excellent) meats. Banks close in the middle of the day, and all transactions are done by hand. Life is very simple along the north coast of Honduras. If you prefer sunshine and tranquillity in an exotic setting, these sleepy beach towns are ideal, and require very, very little in the way of living expenses.

If you want a more luxurious setting, another retirement spot as yet unknown to Americans is the Villa Elena Golf and Country Club, just 20 minutes outside the capital city of Tegucigalpa. This beautiful town sits at 3500 meters in the mountains, and offers safe, tranquil living at a fraction of the cost of a country club elsewhere in the world. A cosmopolitan center on weekends, daily life is slow and the climate is perfect for those who want to avoid the high temperatures of the islands. Here, you can buy either a building lot or a home for around $250,000, with all the amenities of the outside world, including Internet and satellite TV. Located here is the famous American School, which offers a school bus every day.

Getting your retirement residency card in Honduras

Although well worth it, before heading off to seek your retirement paradise in Honduras, you must gather the proper paperwork and head to your nearest Honduran Consulate. It takes about two weeks to start the process, which then is completed in Honduras.

To apply for residency, you will need the following documents:

* Passport, valid for at least one year from the date of your application;

* Birth certificate;

* Police verification showing you are in good standing with the law, and

* Health certificate.

All documents must be authenticated by: the Secretary of State in the state where the document is issued, the U.S. Department of State Authentication Office, and the nearest Honduran Consulate.

You will also need the following:

* Six passport-size photos, and an application for residency, which must be completed and signed before the consul, and submitted along with a payment of $150 per person;

* Sworn statement declaring that you do not belong, and did not belong at any time in the past to the Communist Party (this must be signed in the presence of a consul officer, and submitted along with a payment of $50 per person);

* Sworn statement declaring that you will abide by the laws of Honduras, to be signed in the presence of a consul officer,rr and submitted with a payment of $50.

For each document processed through the consul office, be prepared to pay a $50 charge, which will bring the cost to about $400 per person. For residency needs and questions, we recommend you contact Vanessa Oqueli, at **Garcia & Bodan**, *tel. 504-239-9733; email: jvoqueli@garciabodan.com.hn*, or Italo Tugliani at **Tugliani & Tugliani**, *tel. 504-235-4526; e-mail: Tugliani_corplaw@yahoo.com*.

After you have resided in the country for five consecutive years, you are eligible to apply for Honduran citizenship.

Earning money as a retiree

The government of Honduras offers attractive tax incentives to anyone starting a company that will employ Honduran workers. By doing so, you can enjoy 100% exemption from import duties and income taxes for five years, depending on the size and location of your business.

If you live only on your foreign income, however, you will not pay income taxes on such income, including pensions, regardless of the total amount.

Another option is teaching or acting as a consultant in Honduras. For more information, contact John Coleman, director of **Executive Service Corps**, *San Pedro Sula; tel. (504)57-9128; fax (504)50-6416.* John reports that his phones ring steadily with calls from businesses throughout the country that are looking for advisers and consultants (especially those with American know-how).

Banking

It is next to impossible to cash personal checks in Honduras. And it can also be challenging to transfer funds, especially in the Bay Islands where banking facilities are less sophisticated than the main cities. Many retirees keep money in banks in the Cayman Islands or in the U.S. However, retirees report that local businesses will gladly accept checks from U.S. and Cayman Island banks from regular customers. Opening a bank account can be complicated, especially if you don't have residency status. There are lempira savings accounts and checking accounts, as well as U.S. dollar accounts available. When you deposit a check in your account, the bank will typically not release the funds from that deposit for 15 business days, although once you've established a good working relationship with the bank, they may be more flexible with this time line.

Health care

Honduras offers a high standard of health care, with many physicians trained in the U.S. As you would expect, it is also very affordable. A visit to the doctor costs between $5 and $15, and a private hospital room costs $30 to $40 a day. Complex surgery can be performed for as little as $1,000, minor surgeries for much less.

Pharmaceutical drugs cost about half than those in the U.S. The best hospital along the north coast is in La Ceiba: **Hospital Vicente d'Antoni**, *Apartado Postal #33, La Ceiba, Atlantida; tel. (504)43-2264.* It has modern facilities and many of the doctors and staff members speak English.

In San Pedro Sula, CEMESA medical clinic and hospital is an excellent facility, and is the choice of most Bay Island ex-pats. Most of the doctors speak English, and many are U.S.-educated at universities as prestigious as Yale and Harvard. A full physical is done on the premises, with all necessary technology and laboratories available—for under $200.

Arguably, the finest hospital and medical facility in Central America is the new Honduras Medical Center in Tegucigalpa. This is a full hospital, including emergency services and outpatient services. Every specialty imaginable is covered.

Although medical service in Honduras is excellent, we recommend that you ask for a written agreement before services are performed just to make sure you are not overcharged. Consider the following story as relayed to us: A retiree visited a dentist, who gave him a verbal quoted of HNL1,100 ($85.93) for fairly extensive dental work. But when it came time to pay, the dentist bill was HNL1,800 ($140). Although, the "adjusted" price was still much less than it would have been in the U.S. (about $1,600), we suggest that you ask your doctor or dentist for a written quote up front to avoid any price discrepancies.

In Honduras, you can get health insurance if you are under 61, and a resident of Honduras when you apply. The plan covers up to $2 million in costs and is valid until you turn 70. A local health maintenance organization (HMO) also provides medical insurance. Contact SANITAS, *Mr. Dario Stevez, General Manager, P.O. Box 1801, Tegucigalpa; tel. (504)32-9567,* for complete details on HMO services.

Honduras' best-kept Mayan secret

By Kathleen Means

Many people have heard of Chitzen Itza in Mexico and Tikal in Guatemala, but few seem to know about the other Mayan gem—just a four-hour drive from Guatemala City, across the Honduran border.

The Mayan city of Copán was the southernmost of the great Mayan cities and, like the other ancient empires, it was mysteriously abandoned around 900 A.D. Today, the ruins are a UNESCO World Heritage site, a short walk from the town of Copán Ruinas.

The ruins are famous for their *stelae*—10-foot-high stones carved with stories of the Kings of Copán. Most impressive is the hieroglyphic staircase, which details hundreds of years of Copán history. And although you have to pay extra to enter the excavation tunnels put in by the archaeologists, we found it well worth it—just make sure you get an English-speaking guide, and go early because it can heat up in the afternoon.

We stayed at the Via Via (*www.viaviacafe.com*) for a bargain basement price of less than $15 a night. There are also more upscale, luxurious places to stay—like the hacienda-style Hotel Marina (*www.hotelmarina copan.com*), which has a pool, and most rooms have their own patios in lush tropical settings.

Driving or buying a car in Honduras

To ship a car from Tampa, Florida to Puerto Cortez costs about $600. To ship it from the mainland to the Bay Islands costs about $100. Contact **Jackson Shipping, Inc.**, *French Harbor, Roatan; tel. (504)45-5412; fax (504)45-5599*; or *5353 W. Tyson Ave., Tampa, FL 33611-3225; tel. (813)835-4644; fax (813)835-4667*, or **Hyde Shipping** in Miami *tel (in Miami) 305-913-4923, (on Roatan) 504-455-7564*. In Miami, ask for Juan Llambes, or *e-mail: jllambes@ hydeshipping.com*.

If you're staying in Honduras for a long time, or are moving here, you'll need to apply for a driver's license. Getting official paperwork, such as a driver's license, is often easier on the mainland—this is one area where the laid-back lifestyle of the Caribbean islands can be very frustrating! We feel it's much easier to go to the mainland to do this. In contrast, on the island of Roatan, it often takes several trips to the police department to get a license if the person taking the photographs or fingerprinting doesn't show up. In the mainland towns of La Ceiba, San Pedro Sula, or Tegucigalpa, you'll find everything you need is in one place, and that you'll progress through the system easily.

If you are not a retiree, you must pay duty to ship your car. The duty is extremely high and the system classifies most vehicles in the luxury category; so, unless you're particularly attached to your vehicle, don't bring your car—it's easy to buy what you need. (But note: cars more than seven years old are prohibited from being imported into the country.)

A brand-new Toyota four-door pickup costs about $28,000 in Honduras. A good place to buy a car or truck is from either Avis Car Rental, or Toyota Car Rental. Our people on the ground in Honduras, Ron and Janine Goben bought a five-year-old Hyundai SUV for $8,000, and a four-year-old Toyota 4 Runner for $13,000. Both were well maintained and had low mileage (it's a small island!). One year later, they're still thrilled with the cars.

Habla usted Espanol? (Do you speak Spanish?)

Retirees who speak little Spanish seem a bit left out, to our way of thinking, by their inability to fully communicate. Even on the Bay Islands, where English is the official language, a basic understanding of Spanish will help you make friends more easily. But that isn't to say that you need to speak fluently before you arrive in Honduras. What better place to learn than in an environment where you can practice every day? We met people on Roatan who were learning the language, privately tutored by the local kindergarten teacher, for $1 an hour!

Another alternative is to attend one of the excellent language schools on the mainland. The Central America Spanish School offers flexible classes in La Ceiba, Roatan, Utila, Cayos Cochinos, and Copan. They offer an intensive program, including lodging in a Honduran home, or will tailor a program to satisfy your lifestyle needs and schedules. The course is partly classroom and partly life experience. Contact *info@ca-spanish.com*, or call *504-440-1707*. Their web page is *www.ca-spanish.com*.

Recreation and sports—the perfect environment

As a retiree in Honduras, you will find a range of activities—especially outdoor sports—to keep you busy. You can join the sailing club, or fish for bass in Lake Yojoa, one of the best bass-fishing lakes in the world.

Go deep-sea fishing for sailfish, albacore, or mackerel off the Bay Islands. (To get a fishing license, you need two passport-size pictures.)

The area around La Ceiba is an environmentalist's dream! Pico Bonito National Park, and the nearby Rio Cangrejal offer hiking, canoeing, river rafting, canopy rides, mountain-biking, and climbing treks in wildlife reserves, and horse-riding, either in the mountains or on the beach. Also enjoy the lagoon and mangrove tours, dips in the hot-springs, waterfall hikes, and much, much more. This area is considered the eco-tourism center of the country.

Jungle River is a company in La Ceiba that offers all types of out-door activities and tours in northern Honduras. In addition to all the afore-mentioned activities, this company hosts an adventure tour to La Moskitia, the largest tract of virgin tropical rain forest in the North American hemisphere. A large portion of this pristine area is protected by law under one of five distinct zones: The Rio Platano Biosphere Reserve, the Tawahka Anthropological Reserve, the Patuca National Park, the Cruta Caratasca Wildlife Refuge, and the Rus Rus Biological Reserve. The area is populated by several indigenous groups, of which the Pech, Tawahka, Garifuna, and Miskitos are the most predominant.

The increasingly popular new baseball stadium in Tegucigalpa is a great place to see a game. Not surprisingly, the national sport of Honduras is soccer, and the national soccer stadium is also in Tegucigalpa. In San Pedro Sula, soccer players play at the Morazan Municipal Stadium. Also, almost every town has a field where people play soccer on Sundays.

There is a **Rotary Club**, *(504)37-8459*, and a **Lions Club**, *(504)22-2763*, in Tegucigalpa, and two international women's clubs in San Pedro Sula. Be active, join in, or simply relax on the county's world-class, but largely deserted beaches.

Real-life stories of retirees in Roatan, Bay Islands

Honduras is hardly a mecca for expats—that's why it remains such a wonderful, affordable place to retire. But neither is it the end of the earth. Adventurous souls are already staking their claims in Honduras before the word gets out.

For example, one retired couple we met in Honduras is finishing a two-story house, and renting out the apartment on the lower floor for extra income.

A younger couple we know is not ready to retire, and thus is getting in on the investor's residency program. This husband and wife bought a little over two acres, with sea views for $40,000. They are living on the property now, and building a restaurant, which they plan to open next year.

Another young couple we talked to moved to Roatan with their three-year-old twin sons a couple of years ago. The boys now attend one of several private, bilingual schools on the island, and have a great grasp of both languages. Wireless Internet allows them to keep in close contact with family in the U.S., while also allowing the couple to conduct business online. In fact, there are many people living in the Bay Islands who manage to work via the Internet.

Contacts

International Living's local representatives in Honduras, Ron and Janine, can help you find real estate to rent or buy, put you in touch with a reliable lawyer, tell you about the best places in the country for a relaxing holiday, help you arrange a visa, find a maid, and arrange to ship your belongings. Contact them: **Ron and Janine Goben**, *website: Honduras@internationalliving.com; e-mail: Honduras@ InternationalLiving.com; tel. 1-720-240-4831 from the U.S.* or *cell (Honduras) 504-991-0842.*

Embassies

- **U.S. Embassy in Honduras**, *Avda La Paz, Apdo 26-C, Tegucigalpa; tel. (504)32-3120; fax (504)32-0027.*

Medical

- **First American Title Insurance Company** (Tuey Murdock), *tel. in the U.S. (954)839-2900, ext. 188; toll free: (877)641-6767; fax (954)838-9228; e-mail: tmurdock@firstam.com.*

- **Hospital Vicente d'Antoni**, *Apartado Postal #33, La Ceiba, Atlantida; tel. (504)43-2264.*

Ecuador

Sell your winter clothes, and prepare for the adventure of your life-time. In Ecuador, every cliché you've heard about living large on little money—about settling into the lap of luxury on even a pension-er's budget—is true.

This is one of the world's cheapest places to live. Take $250 out of the ATM Monday morning—and your expenses are covered for the week.

In fact, we ranked Ecuador as the world's best retirement haven in 1999, after it weathered the earlier economic, political, and natural problems during the two years prior, and went on to prosper.

Of course, low prices alone do not make for an ideal retirement or investment destination. There are plenty of places the world over where you can buy cheap land, but where you wouldn't want to live; not so in Ecuador.

In Ecuador, not only can you live on little: you can live very well. Ecuador offers something for everyone, and at prices unheard of in North America and Europe. Golf on breathtaking courses so uncrowded you'll never have to make a tee time. Indulge in a gour-met meal in a world-class restaurant. Why not? The cost is about what you'd pay for bottled water and an appetizer in a restaurant in Los Angeles, New York, or London. Plus, the fresh fruits and vegetables you find overpriced at specialty "organic" shops up north, sell at local Ecuadorian markets for pennies.

It's hard to pinpoint the best reason for coming to Ecuador, but one thing's for sure: this is an affordable—and beautiful—place to live.

Ecuador also offers a high quality of life. This is no isolated back-water. It's a land of opportunity, where a middle class is forming. After waking from a long economic slumber, Ecuador is preparing to join the global economy. Recently, for example, the Quito airport has improved dramatically: it now has new jet ways, a totally renovated entrance, a new waiting area, and is abundantly adorned with huge vases of roses.

From snow-capped volcanoes to dense Amazon jungle, from sun-drenched Pacific beaches to the famous Galapagos Islands, this is a place of astounding natural beauty. Despite covering a mere 0.02% of the world's landmass, it is home to 10% of the world's plant and animal species.

This country's real treasure, however, is its people. Ecuadorians live their lives in jungle river towns, coastal fishing villages, isolated cattle ranches, the grounds of ancient haciendas, and large colonial cities. Its compact size makes it possible to experience many of these different lifestyles in a single day.

It's also one of the few places where a foreign resident or visitor can blend easily into the community, being welcomed into a new circle of friends and a new way of life, with relative ease. As a foreigner here you'll be treated with respect, and the people will be proud to get to know you.

During the past five years, Ecuador has gone through a number of tumultuous changes. Nevertheless, today the country has emerged as a welcoming haven for those wanting to retire or invest here. The property market offers significant bargains. A comfortable lifestyle can be enjoyed in Ecuador on just a fraction of what you'd spend in much of the world.

And remember: Ecuador is one place right now where the U.S. dollar is not losing value. Following the late-1990s debt default, Ecuador decided to adopt the U.S. dollar as its official currency, which eliminates currency risk. Inflation is under 2%, and most economic indicators are positive. Labor costs are still a tremendous bargain, and are not rising appreciably. Property prices, which had been dropping since 2001, seemed to have bottomed out.

Low prices allow greater opportunities

It's not just properties that are affordable in Ecuador—nearly everything is. From the cost to hire a full-time maid to the price of produce, and dinner in a fine restaurant, you'll be surprised at how low the cost of living is in Ecuador.

For example, in the major cities like Quito, Guayaquil, and Cuenca, you'll not have to forgo first-world conveniences. New cars abound—several brands are even made right there in Ecuadorian factories. Everyone has cell phones, and Internet connections are just as common. World-class restaurants serve excellent meals, yet you'll be hard-pressed to pay more than $50 for dinner for two—drinks included.

It's easy to live on less than $17,000 per year in Ecuador, and you can live a comfortable lifestyle while doing it. Many foreign residents have their main home in the city, and also have a country home, a beach property, or even property in another country…a feat that would be impossible on a comparable living in the U.S. Additionally, this low cost of gives retirees the ability to increase their travel, own two cars, or partake in other diversions.

Excellent health care at a fraction of U.S. prices

Ecuador offers access to excellent medical care. In the bigger cities, you'll find hospitals with state-of-the-art equipment, as well as specialists in all fields, and physicians with private clinics. The average visit to the doctor's office runs just $15, with a specialist running about $17 to $20 a visit.

Convenience is another benefit. Daily flights connect Ecuador to major hubs throughout the hemisphere—a flight to Miami takes less than four hours. For those who need to be "connected," Internet cafés are easy to find, and home computer hook-ups are common.

Do you thrive on the hustle and bustle of the city? Or are you drawn to high mountain valleys where cowbells are more common than car horns? Do you crave sun, sand, and crashing surf? Have you always wanted to have your own horse—and ride it into town for lunch?

Your only real problem in Ecuador is deciding where to live, because this place has all these options.

Quito—a beautiful historic city

Quito has been described as the most beautiful city in South America. Spanish influence here is apparent in its stately colonial architecture. Though the city has about 1.3 million residents, traffic is reasonable, except at rush hour and during major road resurfacing projects. The public transportation system, including taxis, buses, and trams, is excellent.

In Quito, we have discovered all sorts of attractive, well-equipped properties ideal for someone interested in city life and perpetual springtime weather. The area is ringed by staggering Andean peaks, providing beautiful views from many properties. The city is in the process of restoring the old colonial center, something that caused property values to rise rapidly in Cuenca and Guayaquil, upon completion. Yet the tremendous value found in these irreplaceable antique homes—many in the $40,000 to $60,000 range—has not yet been discovered by the Ecuadorian investors.

Vilcabamba—our readers' choice in Ecuador

Another hot area, at this writing, is the village of Vilcabamba in Ecuador's southern Sierra. Enjoying near-perfect weather year-round and dramatic mountain scenery, Vilcabamba has Ecuador's highest concentration of *International Living* readers.

Tucked away deep in southern Ecuador, in the heart of the country's southern province of Loja, and bordering Peru, the Incas auspiciously referred to Vilcabamba as the Sacred Valley. Today, it is appropriately known as the Valley of Longevity.

Perhaps Vilcabamba is the real Shangri-La. Plenty of people seem to think so, including a number of young counter-culture types who made it to Vilcabamba in the 1970s as backpackers, and never left. A mellow lifestyle, organic food, and communing with nature were exactly what they were looking for. Today they work hard to ensure that Vilcabamba remains the gentle, pristine place they fell in love with years ago.

And the prices are a dream as well. In Vilcabamba, a two-story, traditional Ecuadorian house with five bedrooms on 2.5 acres, with lots of fruit trees, and a fresh water source, recently was sold to an *International Living* reader for just over $60,000.

Living here is very affordable as well, as the following prices illustrate.

Sample monthly budget in Vilcabamba

* Rent: A one-bedroom apartment in town, $200; a three-bedroom country home, $300

* Utilities: $22

* Phone charges: $20

* Health care: $10 (four $30 visits to a doctor per year, divided by 12 months)

* Clothing: $50

* Car (maintenance and fuel for one vehicle): $80

* Water rates for one family (this can vary by neighborhood): $2

* Eating out (six times per month, with drinks, dessert, tip): $90

* Groceries: $100

This works out to be $574 a month or $18.87 a day to live like royalty in the sacred Valley of Longevity!

The legendary Galapagos Islands

Lying 650 miles off the coast of Ecuador on the equator, you'll find Ecuador's most visited tourist destination, the Galapagos Islands that Darwin made famous.

Composed of 13 large islands and several hundred smaller ones, they enjoy a unique distinction, being home to many types of animal species that exist nowhere else on earth. Ringed with endless miles of white-sand beaches and clear azure waters, they are truly the jewel of Ecuador.

Recent changes in the law have made 3% of the land in Galapagos available for private ownership—with only a tiny 1.5% available for sensible development—while the rest remains National Park. *International Living* readers were the first ones to take advantage of this law, and several have already bought properties. In the past year, the Galapagos Islands have been popular with our readers. Some 30 people have invested in vacation properties in this truly unique environment, where prices once started at as low as $11,800. Today, the asking price is $18,000 to $20,000, and surely that will rise in this legendary location.

Ecuador has become one of the best opportunities we've come across in the last decade for solid, dependable investing in this part of the world. Sure, the economy still has many hurdles to overcome and the politics are a moving target. But we see great opportunity here: for real-estate investment, for business endeavors, and for retirement living. If you have dollars, you have tremendous buying power—and we think your investments in this country will pay off.

The Pensioner Visa in Ecuador

The *9-I: Pensioner Visa* is intended for retired persons who receive pensions from their native countries (pension from a stable source, at least $800 per month). It is also available for an annuity recipient or trustee who will live on cash deposited in the Central Bank of Ecuador, or has income from a trust. In the case of a deposit or trust, the amount must be that which would result by multiplying the monthly minimum over a period of five years. This amount may vary from $800 monthly, and will be determined by the Immigration Advisory Board. To apply for this visa, all the following conditions must be submitted:

1. A visa petition addressed to the Director General of *Extranjería*, and signed by the applicant and an attorney;

2. A completed form "*Solicitud de visa de inmigrante*" for the appropriate visa type;

3. Two notarized copies of an up-to-date passport, with the notary attesting to the fact that its status is legally current;

4. A completed form "*hoja de datos para la cédula*" (a data sheet, subsequently used for your identity card);

5. Two current passport-size photos, in color, with a white backdrop;

6. Visa fee of $270;

7. Retirement documents showing a stable income of at least $800 monthly, certified to be correct by the party responsible for the source of the funds, and authenticated by the Ecuadorian Consul in your country of origin; and

8. Certification by Ecuadorian Consul that the funds are no less than $800 monthly for the applicant, plus an additional $100 for each dependent.

Notes:

- The required income level is subject to change
- Documents must be legally translated into Spanish if not already in Spanish
- These fees are current as of June 2005

Useful contacts

International Living: Ecuador

The staff of *IL* and our contacts on the ground in Ecuador can help with any queries you may have on buying, investing, or relocating to Ecuador. *International Living* Ecuador, *e-mail: Ecuador@InternationalLiving.com; website: www.International Living.com/ecuador*.

Medical

- **Hospital Voz Andes**, *Quito; tel. (593)2226-2142* or *(593)2226-2143.*

- **Hospital Metropolitano**, *Quito; tel. (593)2226-1520; Emergencies (593)2226-5020.*

- **Monte Sinai Hospital**, *Miguel Cordero 6-111 y Avenida Solano, Cuenca; tel. (593)7288-5595.*

Attorneys

- **Maria del Carmen Cevallos**. Maria del Carmen is based in Quito and has handled many real estate transactions for *IL* readers, and we've received excellent feedback. Very reasonable rates, *tel. (593)2255-4193; e-mail: mccv@interactive.net.ec.*

- **Dr. Nelson Idrovo y Dra. Grace Velastegui**, a young huband and wife team favored by *IL* readers. They have become our specialists in matters of immigration and importation. Great rates. *Tel. (593)7284-2225 (office) or (593)7282-0349 (home); cell: (9)611-0451, e-mail: gracevelastegui@yahoo.com.*

Relocation

- **Ecuadorian Transport**, (Gustavo López-General Manager). Gustavo speaks English. Recommended as in-country agents for your international move, *Malearte 654 y Occidental, Quito; tel. (593)2259-2171; fax (593)2259-2172; email: Ecutrans@uio.satnet.net.*

What's in a Name?
by Lee Harrison

People's names in Ecuador follow the Spanish convention, in which two last names are used in formal settings. The first surname is the surname of the individual's father, and the second surname is that of his or her mother. Both surnames should be used when writing the person's name, on letterhead documents, signs, etc. However, people should be personally addressed using their first name and only the *first* of their last names. For example, Carlos Sánchez León, would be called Carlos Sánchez or Sr. Sánchez (never Sr. León).

Women do not change their names when they get married, and retain this same convention. Optionally, they may affix a "de" and then their husband's name to the end of their name, although this is not a typical custom. For example, if Maria Ruíz Cabrera marries Sr. Sánchez, she may choose to write her name, formally, as Maria Ruíz Cabrera de Sánchez. But, personally, she should be addressed as Sra. Ruíz.

A common mistake North Americans make in social settings is to assume that a husband and wife share the same surname, leading to botched introductions later on.

Mexico

Mexico has it all: rich culture, perfect climate, affordable living—not to mention mountains, beaches, deserts, and just about everything in between.

In Mexico you'll find little silver mining towns with winding streets that seem to run straight up into the clouds. This is also where $4 can fill your shopping bag to the brim with fresh fruits and vegetables from the weekly market.

There are fishing villages where boats land in the morning. By lunch, you'll be feasting on giant snapper, sautéed with garlic or simmered in a spicy *diablo* (devil) sauce that you'll wash down with another ice-cold *cerveza* (beer). Or maybe you'll buy the fish right off the boat for $3 (plus the quarter you pay the fisherman's son to carry it home for you), and cook it yourself.

Stately Spanish Colonial cities in Mexico are steeped in tradition, and soaring baroque church spires overlook gracious squares. Here you can dine in elegant cafés, and browse upscale shops on the very spots where the heroes of the Revolution declared independence from Spain and forged a new country.

For all these reasons, and many more, Mexico is one of the world's top destinations for those dreaming of a relaxed and romantic new life abroad. What's more, Mexico has consistently ranked in the top 10 countries on *International Living*'s Global Retirement Index for the last four consecutive years—this year it come in at number four, among the 28 countries surveyed.

As world events, and an uncertain economy, have caused a decline in tourism everywhere. People, especially in the U.S., are spending less money and staying closer to home. They're looking for a simpler way of life in a place where they don't have to give up the amenities to which they are accustomed. They need look no further than Mexico.

With its close physical proximity to the U.S., Mexico enjoys many of the good roads, high-speed communications, and top-notch health care that you'd expect from its neighbor to the north. Those who relocate find it is easy to live and do business in Mexico.

The paradox to its increasing modernity—and its attractiveness—is that things still move a bit slower in Mexico. You can enjoy a relaxed and refreshing lifestyle, like something out of a 19th-century travelogue, and yet it isn't half a world away.

Of course, Mexico is served by a large number of international airports with regularly scheduled flights from all over the world. But imagine having the option of driving from the U.S. or Canada to explore this magnificent country in your own car, at your own pace. Imagine returning to the States and not having to worry about skyrocketing airfare or—perish the thought—disrupted air service caused by strikes, weather or other delays.

Like the other retirement havens of Panama, Honduras and Ecuador, Mexico offers weather, culture, and lifestyle benefits.

First-rate health care at half U.S. prices

You will find that, in general, health care in Mexico is very good, and in many places it is excellent. Most doctors and dentists in Mexico received at least part of their training in the U.S. (and many U.S. doctors have trained in Mexico, notably in Guadalajara). Many Mexican doctors continue to go to the U.S. or Europe for ongoing training.

Every mid-size to large city in Mexico has at least one first-rate hospital. And a big plus is that the cost of health care in Mexico is generally half or less what you might expect to pay in the U.S. The same goes for prescription drugs. On average, prescription drugs manufactured in Mexico cost about 50% less than in the U.S.

Of course, the costs of medical care can vary significantly according to physician, hospital, and the gravity of your condition. On average, an office visit—specialists included—will cost 250 to 300 pesos (about $25). A house call—yes, doctors in Mexico still make house calls—cost about the same. Lab tests cost about a third of what they do in the U.S., and a CAT scan often costs about 25% less. An overnight stay in a private hospital room costs about 350 pesos ($35). A visit to a dentist for cleaning costs about 200 pesos ($20).

A couple can live well in Mexico on less than $26,000 a year

The following list gives you an idea of the monthly expenses a couple might incur while living comfortably in Mexico. We have rounded up the costs to the nearest (U.S.) dollar. This includes a maid (three days a week), who cooks and cleans, and a gardener. Rent is included, but keep in mind that homeowners wouldn't have this expense. In this case you would want to factor in property taxes, but these are rarely inexpensive. (A good rule of thumb is that annual property taxes are approximately 1/10 of 1% of the value of the property.)

Of course, prices will differ depending on where you live. Prices in resort areas, or those with very warm weather that require air conditioning could be higher.

Monthly cost of living expenses for a couple in Mexico:

- Housing (rental of a two-bedroom home): $800

- Utilities (electricity, gas, water): $125

- Household help (maid and gardener, three days a week): $150

- Groceries: $300

- Car (maintenance and fuel for one vehicle): $150

- Entertainment (dining out and other activities): $250

- Healthcare (two people at $240 per year for IMSS insurance, plus $70 per month for private-care incidentals): $90

- Incidentals (clothes, household items, etc.): $100

- Telecommunication (phone, Internet, cable TV): $150

This adds up to a monthly total of $2,115 ($25,380 per year).

But, as we said, everyone's lifestyle requirements are different; you could live on less. It's possible to rent a place for $400 a month (or even less). If you had your maid and gardener service only twice a week, for instance, you'd pay closer to $100 for their services.

On the other hand, if you like to go out to eat frequently, like to travel, play golf, etc., you will obviously spend more money—but still, it will cost you much less than it would to enjoy a similar lifestyle in the U.S.

Hundreds of thousands of North Americans will soon rediscover the investment and lifestyle opportunities still available in Mexico—it's only natural. This means the time is right to get an inside track on the property that could be the home of your dreams.

Whether your dream retreat is a graceful colonial home with lavish gardens, a simple beachfront bungalow where you can prop up your feet on the rail and watch the tide roll in, an expansive hacienda with enough acreage for horses to roam, or a cliff-side villa with sunset views and cool, steady breezes, you are likely to find it in Mexico—provided you look in the right places.

Colonial Highlands of Mexico

San Miguel de Allende

One of the most popular relocation/retirement havens is San Miguel de Allende. At *International Living,* we've been writing about this location for over a decade. Way back when we began our coverage, it was an unsung little retreat, a place artists went to work and live on the cheap, and where we sent our savviest readers to buy up colonial mansions for a song.

The November 2004 issue of *Condé Nast Traveler* magazine rated San Miguel de Allende fourth on the list of top 10 cities in the Americas, only coming behind Vancouver, Victoria, and Quebec City in Canada. In 2005, both the *Dallas Daily News,* and the *Minneapolis Star* featured stories about retiring to San Miguel, as have CNN and NBC News, among others. Suffice it to say, this colonial city has been discovered. With its high-towered church and its curving, cobbled streets, tidy shops selling carefully embroidered linens, and hand-painted plates, homes that belong in the pages of *Architectural Digest,* and lush courtyard gardens in bloom year-round, this city looks like an illustration straight out of a children's fairytale.

The word is out: La Paz is a top retirement destination

The magazine *Money*'s 2003 issue, citing magnificent seaside sunsets, sugary beaches, sailing, diving—and the ability to stretch a retirement dollar—named La Paz one of the best places in the world to retire. Their statistics:

- Average annual high/low temperature (96/54° F)
- Number of U.S. citizens: 3,500
- Median price of single-family, three-bedroom house: $110,000

According to a recent article in *Money* magazine, the expat community in La Paz is small but growing, and new developments—including gated communities—will no doubt bring more. A retiree in La Paz you'll find plenty to keep you busy. Eat out frequently in the excellent local restaurants, take courses at the city's universities and join bridge groups, tennis and golf clubs, there is even a writer's circle. Some residents keep boats at the marina, and just about everyone meets in the friendly town square where you can find live music almost every night.

Housing and daily living costs are much less in La Paz than in Los Cabos, 90 miles down the highway. Of course, La Paz attracts far less tourists than Los Cabos. And tourists in La Paz are more interested in the world-class fishing and scuba diving found in the warm waters of the Sea of Cortez, than in nightlife. The beautiful bay attracts yachtsmen who give La Paz a truly international flavor—plus the city boasts an excellent infrastructure, and phone and Internet service.

The international airport in La Paz offers daily flights to and from the U.S. (primarily California and Arizona). Health care is excellent. People from the larger Cabo area often come to La Paz for treatment. There is much to like about La Paz.

While a lot of the real bargain basement deals in San Miguel are now a thing of the past, compared to anything comparable you've seen in the U.S. or Europe, you'll appreciate the beauty that is still available for remarkably small investments. A three-story colonial near the heart of downtown has been divided into two complete two-bedroom apartments with "killer" views: these are ready to rent at healthy weekly rates of $750 to $800 per week, but are selling for only $245,000.

Lake Chapala

Once a testament to bad ecological planning, but now a renewed and refreshed backdrop to a host of communities on the north shore, Lake Chapala, is home to about 8,000 U.S. and Canadian expats living out their Mexico dreams. The real estate selection in this area is as broad as the lake itself.

In the sunny, flower-laden towns that ring the shores of Mexico's Lake Chapala, property prices are some of Mexico's most reasonable in the "value for money" category.

If you're in the market for a small retreat, a mere $40,000 will buy you a one-bedroom, one-bath condominium in Chapala with a two-way fireplace shared by the bedroom and living room, lots of storage and skylights, and use of the community's pool.

A bit more—$70,000—can secure you a bright, three-bedroom, two-and-a-half bathroom home with bricked *boveda* (vaulted) ceilings throughout, two fireplaces, two terraces, and an inviting garden where banana trees and a rainbow of blooms invite you through the entranceway.

Puerto Vallarta

Where misty tropical mountains wrap arms around the crescent moon-shaped Banderas Bay, Puerto Vallarta is one of the world's top tourist destinations. Puerta Vallarta offers an international airport, pro-tourney golf courses, designer shopping, and world-class restaurants, and it attracts beautiful people from around the world.

It's easy to fall in love with Puerto Vallarta. If you do, you'll be happy to know there are still such places where you can indulge your fantasies, and live happily and comfortably without breaking the bank.

Are you interested in a condo in this elite location, right on the beach? At $95,000, you'll find a place billed the "least expensive" beachfront condo in Puerto Vallarta. This one-bedroom, one-bath condo is compact, but includes security, telephone, parking, gym, on-site restaurants—and one of the world's most romantic views.

The Caribbean Coast—The Riviera Maya and Costa Maya

The amazingly beautiful Riviera Maya of Mexico—the area from Cancún south to Tulúm—constitutes the fastest-growing region in the country. The equally stunning Costa Maya—from Tulúm south to the Belize border—isn't far behind. The government is committed to developing this entire white sand, emerald sea coastline into the biggest tourist destination in the country. Already it's home to several thriving tourist regions. And this government knows what it's doing. Pave the roads, run the electrical lines—they understand—and the tourists will follow. It worked in Cancún. Now they're doing following the same plan on the Riviera Maya and the Costa Maya areas.

Along the Riviera Maya, the 100-mile-long coastal stretch between Cancún and Tulúm, prices are a bit higher the closer you are to the high-traffic tourist areas of Cancún or Playa del Carmen. In Playa de Carmen, for instance, 0.25-acre oceanfront property lots can go up to $900,000, whereas comparable lots in Tulúm go for only $250,000 to $300,000.

Right now, along the Costa Maya, for a 0.25-acre oceanfront property, you can expect to pay $100,000 and up, depending on location, of course.

But is the window of opportunity in this area closed entirely? Well, if it's bargain-basement beachfront you're after, the answer is, unfortunately, yes. But are the prices now on a par with what you'd pay in other Caribbean destinations? The good news is, not yet, but we do predict prices in these areas will continue to go up, and eventually meet—if not exceed—the levels you'll find in comparable locations.

Mérida

Flat-fronted homes, freshly painted (this one yellow, that one green, another one blue, and next door, red), delight the eye street after street. These happy-looking exteriors hide private open-air courtyards within. In this city, 200 miles west of Cancún and a world apart, no building stands over three stories high, with the exception of a hotel or two, and even these aren't skyscrapers. As in Paris or Seville, the scale of the city is inviting—and makes Mérida infinitely "livable."

Mérida is at the true heart of the Mayan culture. It is not only an especially value-packed place to visit, but property prices are among the most reasonable in Mexico.

A colonial home in the heart of town, for example, lists for as little as $59,900. A 15-acre estate outside of Mérida with a seven-bedroom, seven-bath home, a pool, and even a duck pond, can be yours for $150,000.

Wherever you go in Mexico, the people will charm you, the natural beauty will seduce you, and the remarkably affordable cost of living will entice you to stay. Whatever your motives for settling in Mexico—whether you hope to escape the fast pace of life up north, enjoy a better lifestyle for less than you'd pay at home, or discover a safe haven where the crime rate is low and you can enjoy a small-town existence—you're likely to find your ideal home in Mexico. "Beyond Your Expectations"—is the motto of the Mexican Tourism Association. We couldn't agree more.

Contacts

The most important resource you have is *International Living*'s Mexican Office. Our staff is there to answer any questions you may have, or connect you with the resources you need: **International Living Mexico Office** (Dan Prescher and Suzan Haskins, Directors), *e-mail: Mexico@InternationalLiving.com; website: www.MexicoInsider.com.*

Real estate

- For a list of our recommended realtors in various locations throughout Mexico, please see our *website: www.mexicoinsider.com/realtors* or email us at *Mexico@ InternationalLiving.com* for a recommendation. We have personally met those we recommend, and find them to be honest, reliable and knowledgeable.

Note: In the interest of full disclosure we receive commissions for the properties listed in the Mexico chapter.

Embassies

- **Embassy of the United States in Mexico,** *Mexico City consular services, tel. (52)555-080-2000; fax (52)555-525-5040; e-mail: ccs@usembassy.net.mx; website: www.usembassy-mexico.gov/emenu.html.*

- **Embassy of Mexico in the United States,** *Washington, DC; tel. (202)728-1600; fax (202)728-1698; e-mail: info@embassyofmexico.org; website: www.embassyof mexico.org; Washington Consular office, tel. (202)736-1000; e-mail: consulwas@aol.com.*

Financing

- **Collateral International Inc.** (Robin Reyes), *Birmingham, Alabama; tel. (205)951-7337; fax (205)951-7332; e-mail: rreyes@collateralinternational.com.*

Nicaragua

If you're in the market for a place where you can relax and spend a few months a year in a quiet, safe, affordable retreat, Nicaragua is hard to beat. This country offers advantages few other places can match. Its cost of living, for example, is a fraction what it is back home. You can employ a full-time maid for less than $120 per month; spend just $25 on a wonderful meal of local delicacies, complete with wine and dessert; and find U.S.-trained medical professionals who charge $35 for a visit—and who will even make house calls.

To qualify for Nicaragua's retiree program, you need only to be 45 years old, and be able to show a guaranteed monthly income of at least $400. Under this program, you pay no income tax on out-of-country earnings, and you can import your household goods and your car duty-free.

Nicaragua is one of the most extraordinarily beautiful countries in all the Americas. It boasts a dramatic Pacific coastline, long, gentle Caribbean beaches, and volcanoes and freshwater lakes that dot the hilly inland. Colonial cities, like Granada and León, offer visitors a taste of days gone by. Additionally, Managua is rapidly becoming a real first-world city. The country's most famous beach spot, Montelimar, is a 290-room, all-inclusive resort in Barcelo, with four restaurants, an airstrip, and miles of private beaches. Farther south is the popular town of San Juan del Sur, a town where cruise ships dock regularly, and that is quickly becoming a hotspot for North American expats.

Masaya is home to Nicaragua's best craft market, offering just about everything hand-crafted in Nicaragua—ceramics, leather goods, iron work, hammocks, jewelry, rocking chairs, masks, clothing—you name it. With its five active volcano cones at nearby Masaya National Park, this is the best volcano viewing in Central and North America. It's the only place where you can actually see hot magma rising from the depths of the earth—and you can drive right to the top of the volcano.

Lake Nicaragua, the tenth-largest freshwater lake in the world, is famous for having the world's only freshwater sharks. It's great for fishing and, with 350 isletas, for island hopping. The Las Isletas (the Small Islands) of Lake Nicaragua were created in the 1800s when the volcano Mombacho exploded. Today, you can explore this extinct volcano on trails that wind into the cloud forest. You'll see more varieties of orchids in this beautiful spot than just about anywhere else in the world; and all kinds of wildlife, including 170 counted species of birds and Blue Morpho butterflies. The adventurous can take a canopy tour that lets you shoot across the treetops on harnessed zip-lines.

Despite suffering from a serious case of bad press, for the record, Nicaragua is not in the midst of a civil war. This is a nation at peace. Its government is democratically elected, committed to a free-market economy, and is eager to attract foreign investors.

The current president, Enrique Bolaños Geyer, elected in January 2002, is committed to progress and development for Nicaragua. In a 2003 speech, he called Managua the "safest capital in the Americas by far."

Open a tourism-related business—and gain thousands in profits when you take advantage of a 10-year tax holiday

If you've ever toyed with the idea of owning your own B&B, running a sailboat charter, leading adventure treks into the jungle, dishing up meals in your own restaurant, or operating any tourist-related business, Nicaragua is the place for you.

Grocery basket Granada

Eggs: $2.30 per case

Flour: 31 cents a pound

Bread: 84 cents

Milk: 69 cents a gallon

Meat: $2 a pound

Apple juice: $1.05 per can

In September 1999, Nicaragua enacted the most attractive—and most aggressive—tourism-incentive law in Latin America. Law 306 is sweeping in scope and offers hard-to-beat benefits for investors. If your business qualifies, you pay no income or real estate taxes for up to 10 years, and you can bring in (or buy locally) all the supplies you need—from furniture and boats to linens and cash registers—tax-free.

Retire in a safe, welcoming, affordable country

Nicaragua's retiree program is similar to Panama's *pensionado* program in that it offers incentives for retirees. In order to be eligible, you need only be over 45 years old and have a monthly income of at least $400. The country provides significant tax incentives for foreigners, and they encourage investment in the country.

The benefits for Nicaragua's program come mostly in the form of tax incentives. As a foreign retiree, you:

* pay no taxes on any out-of-country earnings;

* can bring into Nicaragua up to $10,000 of household goods for your own home, duty-free;

* can import one automobile for personal or general use duty- and tariff-free, and sell it after five years, tax-free, and

* can import an additional vehicle every five years under the same duty exemptions.

Enjoy Nicaragua's low cost of living

The cost of living in Nicaragua is a fraction of what you're used to paying up north. Our sources on the ground tell us that a two-week supply of pork and beef costs about $65. For enough fresh vegetables to feed four or five people daily for one week, expect to pay about $55. A 30-minute consultation with a U.S.-trained physician will cost you only about $35. You can hire a maid who will cook, clean, and do laundry for less than $120 a month; and you'll spend just $25 on a wonderful meal of local delicacies, complete with wine and dessert.

Below is an estimate of costs for a couple living in Granada. Bear in mind this is city living. If you set up camp in the countryside the monthly cost will be significantly less.

* Housing (rental of a two-bedroom home): $700

- Utilities (electricity, gas, water): $100

- Household help (maid and gardener three days a week): $125

- Groceries: $150

- Car (maintenance and fuel for one vehicle): $175

- Entertainment (dining out and other activities): $200

- Health care: $150

- Incidentals (clothes, household items, etc.): $100

- Telecommunication (phone, Internet, cable TV): $160

That's a monthly total of $1,860.

What not to expect in Nicaragua

By Gail Geerling

Each week visitors arrive in Nicaragua—and to *International Living*'s local office in Granada—expecting to be met with all the conveniences of home. They think grocery stores will stay open late at night, that they'll find 24-hour services, and that a simple phone call will arrange all the details of a new life here in a flash.

After all, despite ongoing efforts, Nicaragua is still a third world country. Bureaucracy and lack of computer or electronic systems make for a potentially frustrating experience if you're accustomed to the efficiency of First-World living. Most transactions here are done manually, from writing receipts to certain banking services.

If your time in Nicaragua is valuable and you want to do something specific—such as see real estate—then planning is absolutely essential. I can't stress this enough.

Shopping for real estate is different here than at home. On-site sales offices at real estate developments are uncommon—as are English-speaking sales staff. In fact, you might not even find so much as a sign on the road telling you where to find the development you're trying to visit. And even if you do find your way, you may be turned away at the gate by a guard with a rifle who doesn't understand that you just want to take a look. If you get past the guard, there won't be brochures handed out as you enter, nor any price lists or other printed information.

If you are serious about shopping for property in this country, you'll need some help. But be careful whom you turn to; real estate agents exist here by the hundreds, but they aren't regulated or licensed.

What should you do to get around these obstacles? That, dear reader, is why we're here. What are you looking for? Our office can help you consider the options after you've answered that question. We can put you in direct contact with developers in this country, according to your specific circumstances and interests. We can even help with hotel reservations and transportation arrangements.

Of course, we do need a little warning if we're going to help you plan properly.

Nicaragua has about 14 national holidays a year, each one usually stretching into a four-day weekend. On these days, everything—except certain coastal resorts and restaurants—closes. Hotels and guesthouses are usually full. Show up during one of these holidays without plans and without reservations, and you'll be disappointed. Also note that weekends are sacred here. Forget about getting anything done from 5 p.m. on Friday until 9 a.m. on Monday.

All that said, the situation is improving. For example, there are now big service stations, such as Esso and Texaco, where you can get fast food or fuel until late at night, as well as larger grocery stores in the cities. Shopping malls now stay open until 8 p.m.

Travelers' checks are rarely accepted. In rural areas, credit cards are useless, and if you're lucky enough to find an ATM—they're popping up in scattered locations—you may also find it has no money or no power.

Don't be discouraged by these words of caution. Nicaragua is beautiful. We love it here. But we've learned to adjust our expectations. We'd love to help you do the same.

The Pacific Coast

Because most of the world still erroneously believes Nicaragua is a country full of problems and political unrest, local real estate—especially waterfront property—is extremely undervalued.

As developers scurry to build along the Pacific coast, the government is rapidly improving the local infrastructure by paving roads and improving tourist areas.

In 1997—when *International Living* looked for land on the Pacific, we found lots for sale here and there, but usually without amenities. Only one "development project" was under way back then. Today, you have several lots to choose from—all with water, electricity, and fabulous views of the surf below. From up here, you can walk to the beach, and drive into town in just five minutes.

Four years ago a parcel of land—with water, electricity, and paved roads—started at $39,000. Now oceanfront lots in San Juan del Sur, with a home, sell from $385,000. However, because Nicaragua is still booming, there are still plenty of new developments emerging and a number of good deals currently remaining along the Pacific Coast.

While it's true that prices are already on the rise, you're not too late to take advantage of some spectacular bargains. At one development we know of, perched up on the hill just outside the town of San Juan del Sur, you can still get land with beautiful views of the harbor and the pristine Pacific Coast...

For instance, *International Living* recommends Rancho Santana* (*www.ranchosantana.com*). An exclusive project developed by our founding publisher will allow you to buy a 1.1-acre lot starting at a mere $40,000. On a 1,700-acre ranch with 2.5 miles of what is arguably the most spectacular coastline in the world, property here is selling fast—and the developers are already running out of inventory.

Laguna de Apoyo Natural Reserve

Lake Apoyo, a proposed World Heritage site, in the Laguna de Apoyo Natural Reserve, formed over 21,000 years ago when a large volcano erupted. It is the largest crater lake in the country, and one of the most beautiful. The views from the top of the crater stretch out over the hillsides to nearby Granada, with a aspect of blue waters down below. Because of its elevation, Lake Apoyo is generally five degrees cooler than nearby Granada, which is only 15 minutes away. Its crystal clear water has therapeutic qualities due to abundant quantities of sulfur and minerals, and it's 85 degrees all year long.

We also recommend to our readers, a choice of three large three-bedroom, two-and-a-half-bathroom villas for sale on Laguna de Apoyo. This development, called Norome,* has homes selling for only $170,000 to $190,000. Each has views of the lake and Mombacho volcano, and access to the lake and all resort facilities (restaurant, bar, two pools, nature trails, conference facilities, massage, jacuzzi, peddle boats, kayaks, and more). Across the lake, one-acre beachfront lots are

*In the interest of full disclosure, *International Living* receives commission from sales at Norome and Rancho Santana.

going for $99,000. The villas are in a rental program and you can choose to rent or build and live on the lots. Lots have access to all resort facilities by special arrangement.

Granada

Charming Granada, perched on Lake Nicaragua, is the jewel of Nicaragua's colonial crown, the second-oldest city in the Americas. Its large central plaza is surrounded by 16th-century colonial buildings, great restaurants, museums, and other entertainment.

You can still find a vacant lot in town in need of renovation, for around $45,000. You can also buy a habitable two-bedroom, two-bathroom house within walking distance of the town center for around $80,000 to $100,000. Fully restored three-bedroom, two-bathroom colonial homes are going for $150,000 and upwards.

The Cadillac of beachfront communities

By Lee Harrisson

I wasn't going to stop here. I shouldn't admit this, but I felt I'd heard all I ever needed to hear about Rancho Santana* back in the days when *International Living* had a sales office there. I came back this time only because my friend Gail Geerling has a home where I could stay while I was in the area (something I'm sure won't happen again once she gets my bar tab from the clubhouse!). I'd been here before, and frankly hadn't been that impressed. Sure, the coastline is beautiful, but, otherwise, I didn't find it really that special.

But a lot has changed in the last three years.

When I arrived in Ranch Santana this time, I was immediately surprised to find myself in the "Cadillac" of the beachfront communities in Nicaragua. I've spent a lot of time in Southern California, and on arrival here I was reminded of the exclusive gated communities near Dana Point or Laguna Beach in Orange County, with their multi-million-dollar properties looking out over the Pacific. Rancho Santana today is also in that category—the cream of the crop—and someday in the future will be priced like Orange County as well.

And it even has more to offer. You wake up here not only to the sound of crashing waves, but also to the roar of howler monkeys and a cacophony of countless tropical birds—and tropical weather you won't find in Orange County, come to think of it. And, as the total property is over 3,000 acres, the views are spectacular and the local environment is secure.

I was also surprised at the number of surfers of my age who reside at Rancho Santana. I knew the surfing here was world-class, but have always associated surfing communities with little shacks on the beach. Live and learn.

Rancho Santana offers a complete array of amenities, and everything's been done in a first-rate fashion. An impressive clubhouse with fine restaurant, high-speed Internet, a new bar, and a beautiful pool looking out on to the beach are just the beginning. It also has a water plant providing pure drinking water, its own cell tower, and all underground utilities. Unlike most beach-oriented projects, you're not "betting on the infrastructure" here, but rather buying into a community where everything's up and running—and it's nice. On top of all this, the monthly homeowners' costs are the lowest around.

I looked at a section called Bella Vista* on my recent visit and found about 60 lots available with awesome ocean views. Bella Vista is back from the beach, but high enough elevation that you can see for miles out to sea. Lots in this area start at just $40,000 and go up to $100,000 for the best 270-degree views. There are other properties available at Santana, but I felt like the best values were in Bella Vista, which also includes some attractive ocean-view wooded lots. Sure, you can buy cheaper on the coast in Nicaragua, but I personally value the fact that you don't have to wonder what things will be like "when they're done."

When Tom Gordon the sales manager and I drove from Bella Vista back to the clubhouse, we startled an eagle that had roosted in an overhanging tree. This was a happy reminder that, despite its growth and fine amenities, this natural environment has been preserved.

For more information on Bella Vista, or anything else at Rancho Santana, contact Tom at *Property@Ranchosantana.com.*

*In the interest of full disclosure, *International Living* receives commissions on referral sales of properties of Bella Vista and Rancho Santana.

Word is getting out about this country. But it's not simply because the property deals are so attractive or the cost of living so affordable. This country boasts a stable democracy, a booming economy, and one of the most comprehensive retiree-incentive programs on offer anywhere.

Contacts

International Living's local office in Nicaragua is working to establish contacts in the capital. If you are interested in property in the area, contact the team at: *Nicaragua@InternationalLiving.com*.

Embassies

- **Embassy of the U.S. in Nicaragua**, *APO AA 34021; tel (505)266-6010, ext. 4641; fax (505)266-9056; e-mail: usembassy.state.gov/managua.*

- **Embassy of Nicaragua, Consular Services**, *1627 New Hampshire Ave., N.W., Washington, DC 20009; tel. (202)939-6570; fax (202)939-6542.*

Medical

- **Clinica Tiscapa** (Dr. Silvio J. Sanchez, an English-speaking physican), *Masaya Highway, one block east of Colegio Teresiano; tel. (505)278-2561, (505)277-1420 or (505)277-1300; fax (505)278-0953.* This clinic comes very highly recommended, and offers specialists in various fields.

- **Hospital Bautista** (open 24 hours), *Barrio Largaespada, Managua; tel. (505)249-7326, (05)249-0967 or (505)249-7070; fax (505)249-7327.*

- **Military Hospital** (open 24 hours), *next to Tiscapa Lagoon in Managua; tel. (505)222-5242, (505)222-2763 or (505)222-2766; fax (505)222-7141.*

- **Hospital Metropolitano Vivian Pellas**, *Manauga; tel. (505)255-6900; website: ww.metropolitano.com.ni.*

Building contacts

- **Chamorro-Abaunza Arquitectos** (Ronald Abaunza), *De Montoya, 1/2 c. al este, Managua; tel. (505)268-1840; cell (505)866-8146; fax (505)268-1841; e-mail: abaunza@ ibw.com.ni or nauticentro@xerox.com.ni.*

- **Rodrigo Carrion**, *tel. (505)267-0417; cell (505)884-6558; e-mail: rodrigocm@tmx.com.ni.*

- **Sorrenti Design Associates** (Hal Sorrenti), *tel. in Canada (519)782-7784; fax (519)782-7785; e-mail: sorrenti@execulink.com; website: sorrentidesign.com.* (Alternatively contact Rohan, *e-mail: sorrenti@globalnet.hn*, at the firm's office in Roatan, Honduras.)

- **Urcuyo-Hernandez y Asociados** (Gabriel Urcuyo), *Del Casino Pharaoh's en Carretera Masaya, 2 c. arriba, 75 vs. Lago, Contiguo Embajada de China, Modulo #1, Managua; tel. (505)277-1227; fax (505)278-8016; e-mail: gut@cablenet.com.ni.*

Croatia

For some, Croatia is a rediscovery. For others it's a first-time experience. Either way, most visitors are thrilled upon arrival. The landscapes of wooded hills plunging into turquoise seas are truly sensational. Apart from in urban areas, such as Split in the south, developments along the coastline are low-rise and low-density. You have to look long and hard for anything resembling a Soviet-style "concrete block land"—on the contrary, the coast and islands resemble an unspoiled picture book.

And they'll remain unspoiled. Last year, the Croatian government issued strict new planning laws. No permits will be granted for buildings less than 300 meters (984 feet) from the sea—and in some instances less than 1,000 meters (3,280 feet). (Obviously, if you're considering buying a plot and building a home, it is vital to ensure all your permits are in order before beginning any construction project.)

The length of Croatia's highly indented coastline totals almost 1,100 miles. But when you take into account the islands, the country's coastline actually adds up to a massive 3,646 miles of loveliness.

This is a coastline that delivers sheer drama. Swathed in pines and cypress trees, carpeted with wildflowers and a herbaceous, aromatic undergrowth, it meanders past medieval walled towns, thousand-year-old little stone churches, orange-roofed fishing villages, and acres of vineyards.

Nightingales sing; hillsides are ablaze with golden gorse, and everybody seems to have a neatly tended vegetable patch where tomatoes, beans, and lettuces ripen in the sunshine.

Onions are so sweet you can peel and eat them just like apples. In orchards, branches are bowed down with lemons, tangerines, and all kinds of soft fruits. For both island hopping and sailing, Croatia easily rivals Greece. Visit any of the islands and it's like falling through a crack in time—a world of stone towns, terraced fields still worked by hand; expanses of untouched forest, quiet coves and beaches…and very few people! Nothing beats dinner under the stars in a little harborside restaurant where you can feast on octopus salad served with freshly-baked bread, char-grilled fish caught that very day, and enjoy a bottle (or two) of the delectable local wines.

Imagine having restaurants like this at the bottom of your street. Even the simplest food invariably tastes scrumptious. Take olive oil—here they often drizzle it over thick bread that's been dressed with chopped garlic and fresh tomatoes, and then grill it until the bread is warmed through. The flavors all combine to give a taste sensation that's truly marvelous.

Unspoiled, relaxed, easygoing, beautiful, and safe: Croatia is one of Europe's loveliest treasures. Everything a discriminating retiree is looking for can be found right here: affordable living, crystal-clear seas, timeless fishing villages, and unspoiled beaches.

Roman ruins, a pristine lake district, and medieval walled cities

Every twist and turn of the coastline in Croatia serves up grandstand views of secret coves, little harbors, and calm turquoise waters. Out in the Adriatic Sea, a galaxy of islands—1,185 of them, of which only 67 are inhabited—shimmer like a cache of emeralds.

What else? Oh, yes—Adriatic property prices are what you could find on the Mediterranean a generation or so ago. Although prices have been increasing at a rate of between 20% and 30% per annum in recent years, (30% in the last six months in the splendid medieval city of Dubrovnik, the hottest spot on the country's real estate map), it's not too late to find great values. Prices are still well below the European average. When compared with many other European vacation destinations, agents are correct in claiming that the Dalmatian coastline still has significant growth potential.

It's hardly surprising, then, that this little gem of a country is experiencing something of an investor feeding frenzy. Where else along Europe's sunshine coasts can you find a two-bedroom seaside apartment for under $80,000? Now could be an ideal time to snap one up since it seems most unlikely that prices will fall. Croatia is seeking accession to the European Union by 2008, though this could actually come as early as 2007.

More about properties and prices in a moment, but first let's put some misconceptions to rest. Although Croatia was once part of Yugoslavia, the vast majority of Croatians actually resent their country being portrayed as part of the Balkans. Both historically and culturally, they regard themselves as firmly a part of Central Europe.

Dispelling common misconceptions

Croatia is not a battle zone. The war here ended in 1995. It is neither Kosovo, nor Bosnia. In fact, Croatia is nothing like either.

If you are under the impression that it's war-torn, backward, poor, or struggling—think again. Such ideas are either out-of-date or misguided. What you need to know is that Croatia is a wonderful retirement destination, a dream holiday spot, and an interesting investment opportunity.

Croatia's geography and historical beauty

To give you an idea of the geography, Croatia is around the size of West Virginia, and covering 21,830 square miles. Shaped something like a horseshoe lying on its side, it basically has three distinct geographical zones: the coastal region on the Adriatic; a mountain region stretching down from the slopes of the Alps; and the Pannonian plain and valley region between the Danube and Drava rivers.

Croatia shares land borders with Slovenia, Hungary, Bosnia-Herzegovina, and what's left of Yugoslavia—Serbia and Montenegro. Straight across the Adriatic Sea lies Italy. In Croatia, you really are at the heart of Europe. From Zagreb, the Croatian capital, Vienna, Austria, is just 234 miles away. From Croatia, Budapest, the Hungarian capital, is 240 miles; Munich, Germany, is 336 miles; Milan, Italy, just 360 miles. From its northern coast, hydrofoils can whisk you to Venice in less than two hours.

The regions within Croatia's borders encompass Slavonia, an extension of the Great Hungarian Plain. To the north of Zagreb, the hilly region of Zagorije may remind you of southern Austria—many of its baroque castles were built during the days of the Austro-Hungarian Empire.

Zagorije is also spa country, touting benefits from drinking and bathing in the mineral-rich waters. The traditions of thermal springs go back to ancient times, when Romans built *thermae* (hot baths) in Croatia. The waters are reputed to be effective in the treatment of ailments such as rheumatism, chronic inflammation, arthritis, and respiratory problems.

In Croatia's northwest, the topmost part of the coastline belongs to the region of Istria. Not far from Trieste, in Italy, this region has been under the flags of various Italian city-states on more than a few occasions during its frenetic history. The Venetians left the most striking architectural legacy, but both Istria's landscape and food have unmistakably Italian overtones, as well.

Moving south, you enter the region of Dalmatia, the "Land of a Thousand Islands." In addition to being home to the wonderful ancient city of Dubrovnik, the region stretches from the town of Zadar in the north to the Bay of Kotor, which lies on the border, and with the new nation of Montenegro to the south.

Large offshore islands such as Brac, Cres, Hvar, Krk, Korcula, and Rab have their own network of towns and villages. The northern islands can be reached from the major port city of Rijecka, south of Split and Dubrovnik. An extensive ferry service links the islands with the mainland.

Relatively few visitors venture inland, though some find their way to the turquoise and emerald-colored lakes of Plitvice National Park. Around a two-hour drive south of Zagreb, the 16 lakes and surrounding forest have been developed for tourists. Boats, trains, and wooden walkways make it easy to keep respectful distance from the full-blooded wilderness experience—including possible encounters with bears, wolves, and wild boars.

Special benefits for retirees

For those who do not receive a salary, consultancy fees, or a similar income in Croatia, the tax situation is very favorable, particularly for retirees. Croatia has no wealth tax, and the following income is tax-free:

* Pensions received from abroad;

* Interest payments on loans, investments, securities, deposits with financial institutions, and similar income;

* Capital gains from trading securities and other financial assets;

* Capital gains from real estate (if you occupied the property, owned it for more than three years, or sold it to your spouse or an immediate family member), and

* Inheritance and gifts are exempt from taxation in the first line of succession. (In other cases there is a flat rate of 5%.)

How to get to Croatia

A number of local airports are served by European holiday charter airlines, but Zagreb is Croatia's gateway airport for international travelers on scheduled flights. At present, there are no direct flights from the U.S. to Croatia. Visitors have to travel via major European airports such as Frankfurt, Vienna, Zurich, Paris, Amsterdam, London, or Rome. From some of these cities, you can also take direct flights to other Croatian destinations besides Zagreb.

You also have the option of going from Italy (whether from Ancona or Bari) by ferry. You can check online schedules by going to *www.jadrolini ja.hr*.

Living in Croatia

Although living costs aren't low for most Croatians, you'll undoubtedly find your dollars stretch quite a long way. We spoke to one couple from the U.K. about the benefits of retiring to a seaside villa in Croatia. They said their annual rates (local tax) bill amounts to about $234. They told us:

"The shops are well stocked. Even white goods (i.e. refrigerators, washing machines) are cheaper than in the UK. We switch our central heating on less than 30 days per season. Between June and September we lead the lives of beach bums, starting the swimming day before 8 o'clock in the morning. We can—if we choose—more than double our pension income by letting our three spare bedrooms to tourists—and we could get a good return on our savings if we were to invest in a roof conversion, to give us another couple of en-suite bedrooms."

Household bills in Croatia

Monthly utility costs generally amount to $30 to $50 for apartment dwellers. Per kilowatt, electricity costs are nine cents during the day, five cents at night. (Electricity is supplied at 220 V and 50 Hz A/C. Most fittings are of the type commonly used throughout continental Europe.)

Water is $1.75 per cubic meter ($1.35 per cubic yard), plus an annual charge of $22 for water waste. Local taxes covering services such as garbage collection generally range from $100 to $250.

Diesel (gas) costs $1.29 per liter. In Dubrovnik, all amenities are within easy walking distance, for those in other areas, there is an excellent transport system in Croatia.

Learning Croatian

You can find a number of language schools through the official tourism website: *www.croatia.hr*. Most local language schools charge $24 to $30 for individual lessons of 45 minutes. Group lessons (40 to 48 sessions) are generally between $670 and $700 for a course.

Five useful Croatian words:

Nekretnina – real estate

Prodaja – sale

Dozvola – permission

Najam – rent

Hvala – thank you

Importing your household goods

Customs regulations in Croatia allow foreigners to import used household goods and personal effects (except for cars) duty-free. You must have owned the goods for more than 12 months.

When shipping to Croatia, you will need the following documentation:

- Passport copy with entry stamp;

- Certificate of residence;

- Work or business permit, if applicable, and

- Inventory

Health care

Croatians enjoy good health with a life expectancy on a par with North America and other European countries. Although fast food places are burgeoning, the country's agriculture and fishing industries lend themselves to healthy eating.

Most food selections in the markets aren't of the mass-produced variety. When you're traveling around Croatia and the nearby islands you'll notice that everyone has something growing—from tomatoes to lavender—in small plots outside their homes. As one expat notes: "really all the market vegetables are organic."

Employed persons and their families have access to state health care, which is covered by government-subsidized medical insurance. However, you will need to pay the equivalent of Social Security to access it. In any case, just about all expats choose to go private.

All major population centers have decent health care facilities. Zagreb is the best served with a large general hospital, Sveti Duh offers seven specialized polyclinics, and 13 medical centers.

Banking

Croatia currently has 40 different commercial banks. The top five are Zagrebacka Banka, Privredna Banka Zagreb, Erste Steiermarkische Bank, Splitska Banka, and Raiffeisesenbank. Internet banking and telephone banking have become typical, and many banks offer products such as kuna-denominated bonds and investment funds.

Throughout the country you'll find over 1,600 ATMs. Credit cards are far more widely accepted than in other former communist countries such as Bulgaria. Splitska Banka (*www.spliskabanka.hr*) offers many of its web pages with an option of English. You'll find sections on retail banking, small business banking, and corporate banking. So long as they have a minimum of $605 or the equivalent, both Croatians and foreigners can open foreign currency accounts, and savings deposits.

Tax-free yachting

European residents who enjoy sailing can make big savings in this country. As Croatia isn't yet an EU member, yachters can legally avoid the value-add tax (VAT) on a yacht's purchase price if its exported out of EU territory. Owners are allowed to moor their yachts in Croatia, indefinitely, without paying import duties. To obtain a residence permit, you need only to have your yacht moored in a Croatian marina. Once in possession of a residence permit, you can sail into EU waters for up to 18 months in any two-year period, without paying VAT on your yacht.

Food

Along the coast, food in Croatia is Italian-influenced; though Croatia does have its own fish stew specialty called *Brudet*. Pizzas and seafood risotto are plentiful. Inland, you'll find more of an Austrian influence, with lots of game and pork dishes, roast duck, veal with cream sauce, and Wiener schnitzels served with potato salad. A pound of rump steak is about $7, and a bottle of excellent *Babic* wine costs around $12 a bottle.

Restaurant (*konoba*) prices vary from place to place, but of course it also depends on what you order. Fish, especially white fish, is quite expensive everywhere. On the other hand, meat is very reasonable, with many mains priced between $7 and $10.

Back to nature

So, you want to stay in a naturist village while in Croatia? Three miles north of Rovinj on the Istrian peninsula, the Monsena village offers 326 bungalows and 341 apartments for "unrestricted sun lovers." On site are bars, restaurants, a coffee shop, supermarket, swimming pool, and kiddies' playground. It's near a pebbly beach (with paved areas), and there are plenty of woodland walks.

Monsena is a well-known venue amongst the FKK brigade. In 1988, it hosted the Naturist World Congress. You don't have to just lay about getting tanned: sports include garden chess, French bowls, windsurfing, motor and sport boating, tennis, table tennis, beach volleyball, basketball, mini golf, darts, cycling, and water skiing.

For a unit sleeping two, prices per person for half board (buffet breakfast and buffet dinner) start at $28 in May and rise to $45.50 in August. Book through **Jadran-Turist Rovinj**, *Vladimira Nazora 6, HR-52210 Rovinj-Rovigno, Istra, Croatia; tel. (385)52-800-376; fax: (385)52-813-497; e-mail: jadrantur-rovinj@jadran.tdr.hr; website: www.istra.com/jadranturist.*

Split and the Dalmatian Coast

International Living can't claim to be the first to recommend the Dalmatian Coast as a retirement destination. That distinction goes to the Roman Emperor Diocletian (AD 245-316), the only Roman emperor ever to retire. He chose to spend his golden years in his palace in Split—built between 295 and 305—where he remained until his death in 316.

In 1979, The Diocletian Palace was declared a UNESCO World Heritage site and it remains at the heart of Croatia's second-largest city. You can walk from the Riva, the palm-lined promenade overlooking the harbor, into the palace complex itself, which sprawls over seven acres.

Diocletian took quality of life and retirement seriously. He spared no expense, building his palace using the white stone from the nearby island of Brac (which was also used to build the White House in

Washington), and importing marble from Italy and Greece for the squares and columns. He even imported a sphinx from Egypt.

If you'd like to live overlooking Split's 1,700-year-old monuments, at the time of print, Croatian Sun is offering a 970-square-foot apartment for $258,000. It's at one of the four entrances to Diocletian's Palace—the Golden Gate.

In the modern part of Split, you'll find plenty of apartments (generally with clean title) for low prices—but we doubt they'd appeal to you. This is one of the few parts of the country that would probably make you think of communism. If you're interested in Split, look primarily in the old town. Here you'll find affordable properties in old (though not ancient) buildings, along pleasant streets, and just a short distance from the sea and the palace.

Rent a lighthouse

Around 55 nautical miles from Split, accessible by ferry or catamaran, Lastovo is a sparsely inhabited island with rocky beaches, miles of walking trails, and an archipelago of over 40 small islands and islets. A local landmark, the Struga Lighthouse, was built in 1839 at the edge of a steep cliff on Struga Bay.

Three generations of the Kvinta family have maintained the Struga Lighthouse. Today they host guests in the lighthouse. Although, there are restaurants on the island, the hospitable Kvintas will prepare fresh fish, and purchase provisions for guests who are without a car.

Mr. Kvinta also takes guests fishing. No guarantee, though, that you'll catch a 39-pound lobster in a fishing net, even though such a monster was netted here at the end of the 19th century. The island fishermen sent it to the Austro-Hungarian Emperor Franz Joseph who thanked them with a large trunk of coffee and sugar. Things obviously grow big here: In the same location, divers in the 1950s brought up a coral tree weighing around 99 pounds!

Another attraction is the Pokland Festival, which has been celebrated on the island for four centuries. During this interesting festival, a puppet is carried through the streets and burned in a ceremony to mark the island's escape from pirates.

Depending on season, the cost of a weekly stay for a lighthouse apartment sleeping two is $525 to $875. An apartment sleeping four is $700 to $1,155. Lastovo and a number of other lighthouses can be rented through *www.Adriatica.net*.

Take note that although few foreigners are buying in Split at this moment, things could change fast if resort prices keep rising. Prices in the city can be as high as $372 per square foot for new apartment residences in elite locations on Marjan Mountain, but the average price is still around $225 per square foot.

In split, summers are warm and dry, and winters are mild. Air conditioning and central heating are necessary only occasionally. Locals, who take advantage of their location and weather, are well known for their love of the outdoors and sport. Indeed, they boast that no city outside the U.S. has a greater contingent in the NBA.

Dubrovnic—Europe's walled wonder

Swifts fly screeching around crenellated towers, past secret courtyards of lemon trees and roses, and waves of russet-tiled rooftops. On the cobalt-blue sea beyond the old port, a lone paraglider drifts toward the island of Lokrum on the sea breezes.

These are the glorious views you get from the rampart walls girdling Dubrovnik, Croatia's medieval showpiece city. You won't find better views of the silken Adriatic, the densely wooded Dalmatian coastline, and the distant smudge of islands, than in this city.

Once a city-state that rivaled Venice, Dubrovnik's history stretches back over 1,300 years. Up until the Napoleonic wars, this was the principal city of the independent state of Ragusa.

Even at street level, it's obvious why Dubrovnik calls itself the "Pearl of the Adriatic." The drawbridge over Pile Gate leads into a marble-paved street called Stradun. Laid out before you is a treasure-house of bell towers, fountains, and palaces. You'll find a Franciscan monastery with one of Europe's most ancient pharmacies, honey-colored houses with deep green shutters, and steep alleyways hiding cozy restaurants, bars, and hole-in-the wall boutiques.

Vehicles are banned from the medieval core—mopeds and scooters included. There's none of that annoying "putt-putt-putt" noise to compete with the pealing of the bells, or the strains of classical concertos spilling out from behind the churches' wooden doors. Most visitors love this car-free environment—it's so refreshing to sit at outdoor cafés without breathing gas fumes or worrying about risking life and limb whenever you step off the curb.

Not only is Dubrovnik more beautiful than you can ever imagine, it is remarkable that so much still remains. For seven months between 1991 and 1992, it was bombarded relentlessly by Yugoslavian army shelling. This wreaked immense damage, but under a UNESCO reconstruction plan, the city has been meticulously restored.

As you might imagine, space in Old Dubrovnik is limited—planners cannot add more buildings to those already within the medieval fortifications. Plus, it has become a hot destination—luxury cruise ships dock every day, and tourists are returning to its nearby holiday resorts in force. The Croatian government is intent on marketing this southern region of the country as a top destination.

Paul Keppler, managing director of the agency Croatian Sun, says Dubrovnik has seen increases of 20–30% in the past six months. Yet even though prices have taken off, property here could still prove a worthwhile investment.

One old town property on Croatian Sun's books is a one-bedroom apartment of 355 square feet, for an equivalent $120,000. That's reasonable—the average price here is around $392 per square foot. You'll generally pay more for houses—usually $500 to $560 per square foot. Croatian Sun has a few properties within Dubrovnik's walls—the cheapest is a bijou house of 650 square feet for $308,000.

You can get a two-bedroom, 42-square-meter apartment in the old town for €160,000 ($193,000). Two-bedroom apartments rent from €455 ($550) to €700 ($840) per week, depending on the season. (For more information on this property, and others like it, contact Iva Zaja of Croatian Sun: *info@croatiansun.com*.)

High rental returns for part-timers

If you want to retire only part-time to Croatia and rent your house or apartment for the rest of the year, below is a chart you can use as a rough guide to determine possible rental returns. Prices are in euro.

Low season: *November, December, January to March*
Mid-season: *April, May, September, October*
High season: *June, July*
Peak season: *August*

Remember: location and property condition have the biggest impact on rental rates.

Type of apartment	Low season per week (April/May/Oct)	Mid season per week (June/September)	High/peak season per week (July/August)	Long-term rental per month
Studio Apt.	$574	$631	$689	$363
One-bedroom	$574	$689	$803	$492
Two-bedroom	$689	$803	$918	$492
Three-bedroom	$803	$918	$1032	$574

Hvar—Croatia's sunshine island

A two-hour ferry ride from Split, Hvar has been credited by *Conde Nast* as being one of the world's top 10 most beautiful islands. Surrounded by sapphire-blue seas, this is an idyll of hidden coves, dense woodlands, and a clutch of quaint towns and villages. As it's basically a long, skinny island, you're never too far from the sea. Home to around 11,500 inhabitants, it's definitely an "in" place—Giorgio Armani and Princess Caroline of Monaco visited last summer.

A low-lying island, Hvar lays claim as Croatia's sunniest spot, based on it getting over 2,700 hours of sunshine annually. Go in late June or July, and wild lavender blooms everywhere, perfuming Hvar's summer with the wonderful smell.

Despite the influx of visitors, the island retains many of its traditions. During Holy Week, for example, a night procession called *Za Krizem* radiates in the circle around six of the island's parishes. It first began as a penitential ritual in 1510, when believers claimed tears of blood were shed from a small cross. Led by barefoot islanders dressed in white, the procession starts on the stroke of midnight.

Hvar's main settlement is Hvar town, a renaissance beauty of 16th-century houses with a harbor, stepped stone streets, and a citadel that once defended the islanders from the Ottoman Turks. The only other sizable settlement is Stari Grad, at the end of a four-mile-long bay on the island's northern side. In Croatian, Stari Grad means "Old Town" and it's a deserved title—the Greeks founded a settlement here 385 BC.

This past summer Paul Bradbury of Hvar Property Services showed us a beautifully restored stone house in Stari Grad (1,180 square feet), with a lush garden courtyard, and emerald green paintwork. A couple of minutes' walk from shops and cafés, this was on the market for the equivalent of $173,600.

House prices seem to be all over the place, but a rough guide for ruins and livable houses is somewhere in the $50,000 to $125,000 range. Going through the fishing village of Vrboska (a kind of "Little Venice" with bridges and canals), Paul pointed out an unrestored house that recently sold for $74,500.

There's a shortage of properties right beside the sea, and the ones that do come on the market command very high prices. Overlooking the blue heaven of Vira Bay, the equivalent of $105,000 is sought for an 860-square-foot, burnt-out shell. Access is difficult—down a steep shingle track—so we had to leave the car up on the road.

Hvar Property Services aims to offer new buildings from $73 per square-foot by this winter. The rough estimate to other island properties is as follows:

- Up to $50,000 for the few remaining complete ruins;
- $50,000 to $120,000 for more substantial ruins and livable houses in need of upgrades;
- $120,000 to $240,000 for restored houses, family homes, and apartments;
- $240,000 and up for more substantial homes.

Some properties cost far more, including:

- A three-story stone house with 1,805 square feet of living space in Stari Grad, $145,200 through Croatian Sun;

- Renovated 10 years ago, a 400-year-old house in the center of Vrboska (Little Venice), is divided into two apartments with separate entrances, plus an attic. The living area is 1,290 square feet, with a 540-square-foot terrace, and a 3,650-square-foot back garden. According to agents Avatar, the garden area can be built upon, but the property as it stands has good rental potential. Price: $211,750;

- On the outskirts of Hvar town, we viewed a 5,370-square-foot house and business opportunity for $1.5 million. In excellent condition, it has owner accommodation with three bedrooms and three bathrooms. The rest of the property comprises six studio/one-bedroom vacation apartments.

Contacts

Embassies

- **Embassy of the U.S.**, *Ulica Thomasa Jeffersona 2, 10010 Zagreb, Croatia; tel. (385)1-661-2200 or (385)1-661-2300; website: www.usembassy.hr.* The Embassy's American Citizen Services unit assists Americans with passport renewal, registration of Americans living in Croatia, birth reports for children of American citizens born in Croatia, voter registration, income tax forms, notary services, and emergency services to American citizens. For consular reports of birth, renunciations of U.S. citizenship, and new citizenship requests, telephone Monday through Friday 9 a.m. to 12 noon for an appointment, *tel. (385)1-661-2272.*

- **Embassy of the Republic of Croatia**, *2343 Massachusetts Avenue NW,Washington D.C., 20008-2853, U.S.; tel. (202) 588-5899; fax (202)588-8936; e-mail: consulate@croatiaemb.org; website: www.croatiaemb.org.*

Real Estate

- **Croatian Sun** (Paul Keppler), *Iva Vojnovica 61A, 20000 Dubrovnik; tel. (385)20-312-228; fax (385)20-312-226; e-mail: paul@croatiansun.com; website: www.croatiansun.*

com. Properties throughout Croatia, though mainly the Dubrovnik area, Split area, and on a number of islands.

- **Sunshine Estates** is a real estate website that passes on queries and makes appointments with a number of agents. Main area of coverage is Istria, the Dubrovnik area and various Dalmatian islands, *website: www.sunshineestates.net.*

Emergency telephone numbers

The following telephone numbers may be useful in case of emergency:

- Police: 92
- Fire Service: 93
- Ambulance: 94

Spain

Picture a sun-drenched whitewashed house with a shady court-yard, perched on a cliff-top in southern Spain. With the deep blue sea beyond, and an olive grove nestling nearby, it's the stuff of which fantasies are made.

Spain is a place of beaches, mountains, fabulous cities, traditional festivals, and of course, guaranteed sunshine. It's not surprising that southern Spain is the most popular country for Europeans seeking a home overseas.

Sadly, most of Spain's Costa del Sol, along the country's southern Mediterranean coast, is overbuilt, and overcrowded with tourists. In many of its beachfront developments, you get the feeling you're in a Florida retirement compound, complete with security guards, fences, and parking garages. The only Spanish people in these places are the maids, maintenance men, and gardeners. It's not a place you want to spend time—unless, perhaps, if you've purchased an inexpensively packaged golf vacation. In short, it's everything we at *IL* try to avoid.

However, there's far more to Spain than golf courses and a concrete sprawl of look-alike apartments—quite the contrary, in fact. We've uncovered several secluded beachfront areas where you can still escape the crowds, and enjoy sunny days along a quiet coast—even in the south—and rent a cottage for less than $300 a month.

What's more, our travels along the Costa Brava (the northern Spanish coast) turned up some equally charming options: affordable property deals in villages set amidst lush olive groves, with views onto a deep blue Mediterranean Sea.

Venture a few miles into the Andalucian hinterland, into the far west, along the Bay of Biscay and along the Costa de la Luz and Costa Azahar. The "real Spain" is waiting for you. Almost unknown territory to foreign tourists, this is where mountain foothills are strung with citrus groves, and where villages cling to a centuries-old way of life.

Plus, we fell in love with Barcelona, a city you shouldn't miss. Surprisingly affordable, Barcelona offers an invigorating mix of traditional Spanish charm and modern luxuries. Galleries, excellent restaurants, and fabulous architecture come together to make this city one of our favorites in Europe, and you can live here for a fraction of what it would cost in most other European metropolitan areas.

Climate in Spain

Spain's climate is mixed: it has a continental climate with hot, dry summers and cold winters in the interior, while moderate, cloudy conditions, with spring and autumn rainfall, are typical on the Mediterranean coast. On the Atlantic coast, the summers are cooler, with fairly heavy rainfall during winter. The Balearic Islands have cool, wet winters, and warm, dry summers.

Language

Away from the popular Costas, English isn't as widely spoken as you might expect. Real estate agents will happily give you listings, but with a focus on local interests, they can afford to ignore the language skills needed to attract international clients. Further complicating matters, most people in Catalonia speak Catalan rather than standard Spanish. Signs don't point to *la playa* (the beach): here it's called *la platja*. Similarly in the Basque Country on Spain's northern Atlantic coast, many people speak Basque.

Barcelona

There's something electric about port cities—and Barcelona is definitely.high voltage. Spain's spruced-up second city has a 24-hour lifestyle, and is popular for weekend breaks with Europeans.

They come to stroll down Las Ramblas with its bird sellers and all-night news-stands; to sip Cava (the Catalan version of champagne) in the Café de l'Opera; to climb the mosaic towers of Gaudi's temple to the *Sagrada Familia*; to wander the Bario Gotic's twisty streets; and to enjoy $10 *menu del dias* in fish restaurants in working-class Barceloneta.

Barcelona is a wonderful city in which to live or invest—there are some splendid residences with high ceilings and parquet floors—but prices are high in central areas. In the Eixample neighborhood, near the Sagrada Familia cathedral, VDH Enterprises has a three-bedroom, 700-square-foot apartment with a balcony, in need of some refurbishment, for $322,000. They also list a recently refurbished 430-square-foot apartment in a quiet area close to the Sants train station, for $200,000.

The Graca neighborhood has become fashionable amongst arty types, but still retains its pleasantly old-fashioned air. Quality homes here are expensive. A four-bedroom, move-in-tomorrow penthouse apartment (1,300 square feet) in a good building can easily fetch $655,000.

The Costa Brava

Situated between the snow-capped Pyrenees and the Mediterranean, the picture-postcard province of Catalunya boasts Spain's most spectacular coastal scenery—the Costa Brava. The name means "Wild Coast," and it's a ruggedly beautiful place of pine-covered cliffs and secret coves. The Catalan countryside has its own special magic: tranquil, green lanes overhung with trees, medieval villages crowned with ancient citadels, and centuries-old farmhouses nestled in the folds of the hills.

Although it's not virgin territory, Catalunya usually gets overlooked in the exodus to the southern Costas. Few people stumble across the exquisite harbor villages around Cap de Begur.

Llafranc, Aguia Blava, Sa Tuna, Tamariu—all are still unsullied by mass tourism. Tucked inside coves of rosy-pink rocks, these are the Costa Brava's hidden gems. Gold, green, and turquoise; the seascapes are absolutely gorgeous. Brightly-colored boats pack miniature harbors, beaches form perfect golden crescents, and the aquamarine waters are crystal-clear. Llafranc and Tamariu are intimate harbor villages with small clusters of whitewashed *residencia*—apartments climbing the pine-clad hills. Both have golden arcs of sandy beach, tree-lined promenades dotted with terraced cafés, and coastal paths.

During winter, the upturned sailing boats beached on its strand look just like a school of brightly-colored miniature whales.

The asking price for a three-story Tamariu village house is $380,000. The three-bedroom, two-bathroom house is 980 feet from the beach. It has two bright and airy terraces from which to enjoy the views. This home is being sold through Costa Brava Homes.

Begur is the best place to start looking for properties around Llafranc and neighboring villages. Three miles from Aigua Blava on the coast, this medieval hilltop town has wonderful views of a splendid castle and the sea, from its *mirador* viewpoint. If Begur takes your fancy, a pretty modern house, with three double bedrooms, a terrace and a private garden, within walking distance of town, is $285,000 through Domus. In surrounding *urbanizations* (suburbs), you can find homes with around 1,075 square feet of living space from $250,000.

Another likeable part of the Costa Brava is Palamos, and its satellite villages of Sa Forsa and Sant Antoni de Calonge. This area is more central, and Barcelona is located within easy commuting distance, just over an hour away on the Autopista. Also see Palamos, a small town with a working port, evening fish market, and a housing market that's mostly local.

Beyond the Costa—Rural Andalucia

For a taste of a more authentic Spain, the hills behind the Costa del Sol's busy resorts and golf course condominiums turn up plenty of treasures. Here you'll find centuries-old, whitewashed villages—the famous *pueblos blancos* (white houses). Steeped in the remains of their Moorish past, they cling like limpets to the steep hillsides.

Magical places to go house hunting include the 31 towns and villages of the mountainous Axarquia area, high in the foothills above Malaga. No mass tourism, no high-rise hotels mar this landscape. Instead, you find a timeless scene of orange groves, and avocado pear plantations, where mules and oxen remain in everyday use.

Granada

Baking under Andalucian skies, Granada pleasantly taps into the emotions as well as the senses. It bridges the worlds of Islam and Christianity, meshing together Jewish and Gypsy traditions along the way. With the Sierra Nevada mountain range as a backdrop, it's difficult to envisage a more dramatic setting for a city, or a sultan's palace...

Most foreign buyers are beguiled by the "wow factor" of Granada's compact center. According to Antonio Carrasco of Oasis Inmobiliaria, newly–built, and recently restored properties in central Granada mostly range from $360 to $720 a square foot.

Defeated by 13 morcillas

By Steenie Harvey

La Alpujarra is a heart-stoppingly lovely region of Spain's Granada province. I'm staying in a rustic hotel called Finca los Llanos in Capileira, in a village that perches at the top of a gorge that's a giddy 5,000 feet above sea level. From Capileira you can follow the gorge down to the villages of Bubion and Pampileira, or strike out along forest tracks towards Pitres and the Taha Valley. And if you're feeling really energetic, you can tackle Mount Mulhacen's 11,000 feet.

The mountain air will give you an appetite, but make sure you come with a good phrase book. Translations in English are often baffling (if you know what "hoar frost rime to the table" is, you're better informed than I). Year-round, the locals enjoy feasting on hearty fare more suited to winter. Menus feature stews of venison, goat, or wild boar; rabbit; snails with rice; plates of local cured hams, and sausages. Here *sopa de ajo* is not a blessedly chilled soup of garlic, cream, and almond like in Granada or Seville. In the Alpujarra, *sopa de ajo* is hot garlic soup spiked with chopped fried eggs and chunks of ham.

Without knowing what it was, earlier I'd opted for a lunchtime Alpujarran Platter. It turned out to be a weird variation of an Irish breakfast: ham, sausage, fried eggs, blood pudding, and potatoes cooked with red and green peppers.

I'm not sure fried eggs mix well with wine, but the sausage-shaped blood pudding was particularly tasty. Now I realize that some readers may find the idea strange, but I'm extremely partial to dishes of congealed pigs' blood. (If your stomach is heaving in disgust, be sure to spurn all Spanish dishes that contain the word "*morcilla*.") But anyway, tonight in the Ruta las Nieves hostelry I'm going for a full plate of *morcillas*. And here it comes...

> Good grief! Does the waiter really expect me to tackle 13 blood pud-
> dings? Seems so. Costing €6 ($7.30) for the entire plateful, each chunky
> pudding is about four inches long. The first five are succulently good.
> Getting through the sixth starts to become a major struggle. I give up on
> the seventh. Even washed down with a €4.40 ($5.40) jug of local wine, I'd
> guess the hungriest hiker has never managed to finish them all.

As an alternative to these high prices, we favor locations on Alhambra's slopes in downtown Granada. Also lovely are the hilly Albaicin and Sacromonte neighborhoods. Houses of around 1,300 square feet occasionally surface for less than $265,000 in the Albaicin, but they sell quickly. And at this price, an Alhambra view is unlikely.

Cost of living

Living costs in Spain are fairly low, even in cities. Leaving aside rent or mortgage payments, a couple could enjoy a reasonably nice lifestyle for approximately $23,000 yearly—while eating out regularly.

Once you know where to go, a meal for two with wine can cost as little as $40. For the best value, choose the lunchtime *menu del dia*—the menu of the day. Although the food is likely to be more filling than fancy, there's normally a choice of dishes on the three-course lunchtime menu.

In most places, the *menu del dia* will cost between $11 and $17. A local beer and a tapa (a little snack, which can be anything from a couple of rings of fried squid to a slice of ham topped with an olive) costs around $1.80. Even dining in classier restaurants isn't overly costly. For a couple, the bill is usually somewhere between $45 and $70—wine included.

Grocery bills are hard to estimate, but the following short list will give you some idea of costs:

- Milk (one liter): 77 cents
- Coca Cola (two liters): $1.50
- Bread (300g): $1.55
- Large eggs (dozen): $1.45

- Camembert cheese (250g): $2.64

- One bottle of local wine: $3.47

- Potatoes (5 kg): $1.55

- Chicken breasts (1 kg): $7.95

- Tomatoes (1 kg): $1.23

- Bananas (1 kg): $1.97

- Prime steak (1 kg): $26.42

- Swordfish (1 kg): $34.29

- Coffee (Nescafé 100g): $3.14

You can go to the cinema for $4.50–$6.50, and get a mid-range seat in the shade at Madrid's bullfighting arena for $31.80 ($3.50 for a seat high up in the sun.)

Health care

Unlike 25 years ago, there is no shortage of good hospitals and private clinics along the southern Costas. However, costs for private health insurance vary enormously—though you're likely to find it far more affordable than at home. Basic policies for the 55 to 60 age group start at around $640 annually, and go up to around $2,600 for a comprehensive plan. A routine visit to a private doctor is normally $40 to $60.

State health provision is also considered good, and is available for free or at reduced costs. However, you must be contributing to Spanish Social Security or be receiving a state pension from another EU country to benefit.

Contacts

Real estate

- **Agencia de Serveis Immobiliaris Domus**, *Creu 23, Begur, 17255 Girona; tel. (34)972-622072; e-mail: domus@domusbegur.com; website: www.domusbegur.com.*

- **Casa Home Search**, *Trav de Dalt, 26, 08024 Barcelona; tel. (34)654-371455; e-mail: info@casahomesearch.com; website: www.casahomesearch.com.*

- **Domicil Costa Brava Sl**, *Passeu del mar C. Josep Mundet No. 18, Edifica Laura, Sant Antonio de Calonge, Girona; tel. (34)972-6614-87; e-mail: info@domicilcostabrava.com; website: www.domicilcostabrava.com.*

- **Venasierra**, *"Cerro de la Reina" nivel 1 – no 15, 11630 Arcos de la Frontera (Cadiz); tel. (34)956-700-109; e-mail: venasierra@venasierra.com; website: www.venasierra.com.*

- **La Segur Agencia**, *Nuestra Senora de la Oliva 19, 1150 Vejer de la Frontera (Cadiz); tel. (34)956-451-082; e-mail: lasegur@wanadoo.es.*

Insurance

- **PHA Expat**, *89 Station Road, Sidcup, Kent DA15 7DN, United Kingdom; tel. (44)870-7700-946; fax (44)208-309-2909; e-mail: expat@phauk.com; website: www.phaexpat.com.*

- **BUPA International**, *Russell Mews, Brighton BN1 2NR, United Kingdom; tel. (44)127-332-3563; fax (44)127-386-6583; website: www.bupa-intl.com.*

Medical

- **Hospital Costa del Sol**, *Ctra. Nacional 340 Km 187 29600 Marbella; tel. (34)9528-28250 or (34)9528-62748; e-mail: info@hcs.es.*

Italy

If you've never been there, go! Italy is one of those places that warms the heart, and satisfies the stomach! And once you *have* been there, you're always looking for reasons to go back. Imagine being able to spend every springtime in Rome or Venice or Florence—can't you just picture yourself meandering beside the Arno river on a perfect May evening when all the terracotta roofs and ancient palaces are bathed in that special Florentine glow? But you don't have to spend all your time in Florence or any of the other great art cities to experience the magic. Italy's landscapes are as gorgeous as they are diverse. Historic walled towns, timeless villages crowning dozens of little hilltops like tiaras, and fields covered with bright yellow sunflowers. Gnarled olive groves, and lemon, orange, and almond trees, golden beaches and jewel-like Alpine lakes are found throughout the country. Discover romantic, mysterious islands, smoldering Mount Etna, or the glittering peaks of the snow-covered Alps and the Dolomites.

The Italian Lake district is admittedly well trodden, but what do you know about the islands of Sardinia and Sicily? Or of Le Marché, an exquisite region on the eastern coast that shares the same luscious Renaissance landscapes as Tuscany and Umbria, but where properties are much more sensibly priced? Or of Apulia far in south, a languid land of olive trees fringed by the turquoise Adriatic Sea, and noted for its curious dome-shaped *trulli* houses?

Are you dreaming of a 3,000-square-foot restored farmhouse with space enough for all your family and friends, or an unconverted farmhouse or villa that you can do up and then run as a B&B? Or perhaps you picture yourself in a cozy village house just big enough for two, or else a home overlooking the *piazza* (square) of a small historic hill town. Does a villa beside the looking glass Northern Lakes appeal to your imagination? How about an apartment on the Mediterranean or Adriatic coast...or in a major city such as Rome, Florence, or Venice? Perhaps the rolling fields and hillsides crowned with castles appeals to your tastes or, maybe, the excitement of the city. Whatever your dream, Italy can make it come true.

Although the best areas of Rome, Florence, and Milan are admittedly expensive, some regions are more affordable than you might expect. In rural areas and small towns, plenty of homes are on offer for as little as $100,000—and often a lot less.

Health care

As far as health care is concerned, Italy ranks among the World Health Organization's top 10 countries for quality health services. By contrast, the U.S. only holds 37th place, despite being the highest spender. However, although medical facilities are considered to be adequate for any emergencies, many public hospitals are overcrowded and under-funded.

Italy has a national health plan (*Servizio Sanitario Nazionale*), which provides for hospital and medical benefits. U.S. and Canadian citizens who are legally resident in Italy can apply to join the plan. Eligibility for the plan depends on certain criteria, i.e. your nationality, work permit, etc.

If you are a resident of Italy and covered by the national health plan, hospital services will be provided to you and your dependents, free of charge. Visitors, or persons not enrolled under such a plan, are expected to pay full hospital charges and then claim a reimbursement from their insurance provider. In case of an emergency, head for the nearest hospital.

Tax-free shopping in Italy

According to Global Refund (formerly European Tax-Free Shopping), almost two-thirds of American travelers don't realize they can claim VAT (sales tax) refunds on the purchases they take home.

Non-EU citizens (but only non-resident visitors) are entitled to claim back the sales tax paid on many items sold in many Italian stores. Just fill out your tax-free shopping checks as you shop—and you will get your tax rebate either in cash, by check, or by credit card refund.

The two main companies specializing in refunding sales tax are Cashback and Global Refund. Numerous shops and outlets in Italy are connected to them: large department and chain stores, small craft shops, hotel boutique shops, and specialty outlets such as record shops, sports stores, etc.

Some shops can give you a tax refund at the point of purchase. However, you still must fill in the tax-free shopping checks. If the store isn't geared up for refunds, either cash them in at the refund desks at the airport, or mail them back within 90 days. If checks are not returned within 90 days of purchase, you'll be charged the full amount of VAT on your credit card.

If you don't have time to go to the companies' refund desks at the airport, get your vouchers stamped at customs as you leave, then freepost the company the checks in their international pre-paid envelopes to receive either a cash, or credit card refund. See *www.cashback.it* and *www.globalrefund.com* for more information.

Elective Residency Visa

This is the type of visa generally used by foreigners who are retired, and can collect income from a retirement or pension plan.

To obtain an Elective Residency Visa, you must apply in person to the specific Italian consulate that covers your jurisdiction before leaving home. The documents you will need are:

- A current passport valid for at least three months beyond the validity date of the visa requested, with a blank page available for the visa to be affixed;

- If you are not a U.S./Canadian citizen, an Alien Registration Card;

- Visa Application Form, duly completed and signed in the presence of a Consular Officer;

- One recent passport-size photograph (2 x 2 inches in size, full face, front view, color);

- A letter from the applicant detailing the reason for his/her stay in Italy, duration of stay, where he/she plans to reside, and name of persons accompanying the applicant such as spouse and children;

- Proof of financial means such as original financial statements from banks, investment/brokerage firms, Social Security, etc., indicating current balances (such balances cannot be derived from current employment or other work activities—in other words, you cannot finance your residence in Italy through work);

- Certificate of good conduct (police record) issued by the local police authority or by the FBI field office;

- Rental agreement or deed for property in Italy, and

- Proof of valid medical insurance (translated and stamped by the Italian Consulate).

At the time of writing, a processing fee of $62.50 must be paid in cash. (This may change as the exchange rate gets adjusted every three months.)

For each document you submit, supply the original and a photocopy. According to the Italian consulate, visa-processing times vary between two and 15 days. A Residency Visa is issued solely to those who are planning to move to Italy. It does not allow the applicant to work.

Although U.S. citizens are unlikely to experience problems, having a Residency Visa does not automatically guarantee you entry to the country. The Italian consulate advises that travelers carry copies of the documentation they submitted when applying for the visa, particularly those showing financial means.

Rome

The Vatican, the Forum, the Trevi Fountain, the Colosseum, the Arch of Titus, the Castle of St. Angelo, and the Aurelian Walls—with more than 2,600 years of history and culture, the whole of the city of Rome has been likened to a museum. This museum also has elegant shopping areas, green parks, and arguably Italy's most vibrant lifestyle.

Rome's variation in property prices is enormous: $235 to upwards of $1,120 per square foot. Apartments in refurbished buildings in decent, centrally located, residential neighborhoods, are mostly somewhere between $370 and $515 per square foot. At the $235 per square foot level, you're likely to be beyond the inner city—somewhere in the sprawling mass of high-rise suburbs. As many of these areas are run-down, they are only for the brave-hearted home-buyer.

Beyond the activity of the inner city, you'll find some very exclusive residential areas—beyond the Catacombs on the Appian Way for example. Though villas in this area are lovely, the prices are astounding—generally over $2 million.

Le Marché

Hills topped by medieval castles and tiny walled towns glowing in warm shades of pink, ochre, and gold...a green and unspoiled land-scape of stone farmhouses, olive trees, and vineyards...a blue sea and endless miles of golden beaches. Pronounced "lay markay," Le Marché means border country. Here the country's Renaissance landscapes hem the hot southern provinces of the Mezzogiorno, the realms of the mid-day sun.

Try imagining over-valued Tuscany without the crowds, and with lower prices—that will give you an inkling of what Le Marché offers. Along with lovely landscapes, there's probably enough art, culture, and history in Le Marché to keep most folks occupied for a lifetime. The area's facts and figures are astounding: over 1,000 important monu-ments, 106 castles, 33 fortresses, 163 sanctuaries, 40 abbeys, and more than 100 little towns classed as "art cities."

At the time of going to print, Viviun lists a three-bedroom, restored 16th-century, stone townhouse with a garden in a Le Marché village for $167,000.

(Warning: Be aware that the hill towns in Le Marché aren't ideal if you're not fond of walking a great deal.)

Calabria

The aim of Calabria's "Revitalization Projects" is to restore 1,000-year-old walled cities to their original splendor and to make the area a haven for artists, writers, and people in search of *la dolce vita* (the good life). The concept isn't totally new to Italy. Virtually abandoned by tourists 50 years ago, today Ravello and Positano on the Amalfi coast rank among the world's top travel destinations. Similarly, small towns in Tuscany have been revitalized.

Now it's Calabria's turn. Badolato, established in 1,080 AD, perches on a hilltop overlooking the crystal-clear Ionian Sea. In a valley above the coastline, Torre di Ruggiero's history dates back to 800 AD. Surrounded by olive, orange, lemon, hazelnut, walnut, and chestnut groves, both settlements are in southern Italy, on Calabria's Ionian coastline. And they're at the center of one of Europe's most unique revitalization projects.

In order to attract tourism, as well as stimulate the local economy, Calabria's regional government has introduced a "back to life" initiative. *Palazzos* (palaces) and ancient villas are being restored to their former glory. Village streets have been repaved to resemble the original cobblestones; new roads, plumbing, and electricity have been installed as part of a continuing program to completely renovate the infrastructure for new residents. One of Badolato's palazzos is being transformed into a luxury hotel, international library, and museum.

Eating out in Calabria is cheap. Full-size pizzas from a traditional wood-fired oven cost between $4 and $6. Seafood risotto studded with clams, mussels, shrimp, and octopus averages $9; *pesce spada* (swordfish) is $9.50. A jug of house wine is about $3.50, bottles of good varieties are about $9.

At the time of going to print, KeyItaly offers a three-story house in the old center of Santa Maria del Cedro in Calabria (in need of renovation) for $33,500. It has superb views out over the blue Mediterranean from its elevated position.

A&M Immobiliare has a two-bedroom condo apartment close to the beach in Scalea with a small and a large terrace, canopy, condo and parking for $65,000.

Cost of living

Generally speaking, living in Italy can be quite inexpensive if you learn to adapt to a European lifestyle, which is probably healthier in any case than living in the U.S. If you reduce or avoid consumption of imported U.S. products—American sodas etc., and eat local produce, for example.

Electricity is expensive but it is also true we have longer days and fewer electrical appliances. Central heating is kept at lower temperatures, and from Rome southwards, heat is really only necessary for one to four months a year. Most regions where heating is necessary, use gas heating as it is cheaper.

In the small city of Lazio (near Rome) a yearly budget for a family of two is given as follow:

Two-bedroom apartment for long-term contract (over two years) costs $900

Gas: $208.33

Electric: $50

Water: $12.50

Phone: $50

Garbage collection: $12.50

Food: $433.33

Health: $83.33

Entertainment (dinner out one night a week—cinema or theatre another night same week): $333.33

Maid once a week $183.333

That's $74.50 a day for a couple. A budget in Le Marché works out about the same as here. Heating may cost a little more.

Calabria is a lot cheaper (30% to 50% in most fields).

A "Trulli" Great Opportunity
By Maryalice Wood

In the Puglia region of Italy's boot, on a road less traveled, you'll find the small city of Alberobello. Don't pass it by! On first sight of the unique

---

domed dwellings here, you'll think you're caught in a time warp or fairytale.

The history of this magical area goes back to the 16th century. Originally the *trulli*—mortarless limestone buildings with characteristic domed or conical roofs—were erected as temporary homes for local farmers. Temporary, because feudal landowners abused their powers by chasing away settlers whenever the king came to inspect their holdings. You see, the more dwellings on their land, the more tax they had to pay. Whenever news arrived that the king was coming, down came the trulli. Maybe not the first attempt at tax evasion, but certainly a creative one.

As you can imagine, the farmers colonizing this area got fed up with this way of life and bravely appealed to their king. He listened to their plea, and declared the village of Alberobello free on the May 27, 1797. From then on, trulli were built with mortar, but fortunately the old tradition of pyramid-shaped roofs built out of corbeled limestone slabs didn't change.

As we wandered up and down the hills of Alberobello, the historic charm as well as the Mediterranean sun warmed us. We toured a few of the trulli open for business—gift shops, hotel lobbies, restaurants, and offices. But many of these *trullo* dwellings remain just that—homes. And the signs are up: "Trullo For Sale Or Rent."

Purchase prices are reasonable, depending on the state of repair, or disrepair of the trullo. Like us, you just might fall in love with the unique elfin domes, and the old-world ambience of this Italian city of 10,000 friendly inhabitants. If you're curious, check out the trulli for yourself...then dream of renting or buying your own piece of history.

Contacts

Based in Florence, *International Living*'s "woman in Italy" is Carol Milligan—a resident of 32 years. Carol is an experienced realtor and a member of FIAIP. Whether you're looking to rent, buy, or take a vacation in the Florence area, we urge you to make Carol your first port of call, *e-mail: Italy@InternationalLiving.com; website: www.italy-rentals.com* or *www.vacations-in-italy.com.*

Real estate

- **Domenico Leuzz**i, *Costa degli Angeli, Corso Umberto 1, Badolato (CZ) Italy; tel. (39)0967-815-807; e-mail: coastofangels@virgilio.it; website: www.intercomm.it.*

- **Lois Allan**, *Immobiliare L'Architrave, Piazza Giarella 4, Monti, Licciana Nardi 54017 MS, Italy; tel. (39)187-472-068; e-mail: loallan@tin.it; website: www.larchitrave.it.*

Italian realtors are called *immobiliari*, and over 15,000 of them belong to FIAIP (Federazione Italiana Agenti Immobiliari Professionali). Contact them for names and addresses of agents in your chosen area, or check out their website: *www.fiaip.it*. Although it's in Italian, all member agents are listed on the site. (Just click on the map of Italy to find the addresses of ones in your chosen region.)

- **FIAIP (Sede Nazionale)**, *Piazzale Flaminio 9, 00196 Roma; tel. (39)06-321-9798; fax (39)06-322-3618; e-mail: fiaip@fiaip.it.*

Medical

- **Salvator Mundi International Hospital**, *Viale Mura Gianicolensi 67 (near the Vatican); tel. (39)06-588-961.*

- **Rome American Hospital**, *Via E. Longoni 69; tel. (39)06-22-551.*

- **Dei Glicini e Ulivella**, *Via Pergolino 4/6, Florence; tel. (39)055-416-081.*

- **Villa Maria Beatrice** (Cardio-vascular Surgery), *Via Manzoni 12, Florence; tel. (39)055-23571.*

- **American International Medical Center**, *Via Mercalli 11, 20122 Milano; tel. (39)02-5831-9808; fax (39)02-5831-6605; e-mail: wfreilich@iht.it.*

- **The Milan Clinic**, *Via Cerva 25, Milano; tel. (39)02-7601-6047; e-mail: drjames@compuserve.com.*

Embassies

- **U.S. Embassy**, *Via Vittorio Veneto 119A, Rome 00187; tel. (39)06-46741; fax (39)06-4882-672; website: www.usembassy.it/mission.*

Thailand

Thailand—the only country in SE Asia never to be colonized—has a romantic heritage that always beguiles visitors: from the razzle-dazzle of Bangkok, to the floating markets and silk emporiums. The northern heartland offers misty mountains and paddy fields; hill-tribe villages and hot springs; dragon-necked temples and night bazaars overflowing with curios. Then there's the coast and islands, with their salt-white sands and translucent blue-green seas.

Thailand offers a stable government, a friendly population, and some pretty solid fundamentals: Investors garner steady rental returns. Expats enjoy low living costs coupled with western comforts.

Although Thailand is a developing country with a low-wage economy, it also has its charms. Sure, much is exotic or downright strange to western eyes: slow-moving water buffalo and electric-green rice fields, Buddhist shrines and spirit houses, "Ladyboys" and toothless, Akha tribeswomen, outdoor tailors with old-fashioned sewing-machines, food-carts selling snacks of deep fried grass-hoppers, elephants roaming busy city streets.

On the other side of the coin, are glittering steel-and-glass sky-scrapers, air-conditioned shopping malls, luxury condos, and super-sized supermarkets stocking western brand goods. In Thailand, the laidback lifestyle really does come with home comforts.

In locations favored by expats, most people speak English. These communities have top-class hospitals with American-trained doctors —and international schools, too. You'll find golf courses and "swish" marinas, skinny lattes, and not-so-skinny cheeseburgers, restaurants running the whole gamut from Italian to French to Mexican.

Chang Mai

Thailand's arts and crafts center, Chiang Mai, was founded in 1296. All golden wats (temples), teakwood houses, and dragon sculptures, this is what we call "traditional Thailand." This land is a patchwork of misty hills, rice-fields and jungle, and the city's surrounding province is home to numerous hill-tribes.

Visitors adore Chiang Mai. Enclosed by a moat, its old quarter is a beguiling warren studded with temples and craft workshops. Artisan traditions go back centuries. Major draws are textiles, teak furniture, silver-smithery and metalwork, woodcarving, lacquerware, paper-making, and ceramics.

But Thailand isn't just the place to get your fill of elephants, hill-tribes and markets—it's also where to find charming homes at astonishing prices. It's still possible to buy attractive two-bedroom homes here for under $50,000.

Two must-dos in Bangkok

Bangkok is a huge sprawl of over six million inhabitants. Everything you've heard about its bargain-price tailoring and cheap eats is true— although stories of traffic jams, pollution, and the seedy sex trade aren't exaggerated either. It's not an easy capital to fall in love with, but spend a couple of days here. When the noise and traffic becomes too much, I recommend taking a long-tailed boat along Bangkok's scenic backwaters on a *Klongs* and *Wats* (Canals and Temples) tour. You can do it yourself—hiring a long-tail boat along the Chao Phraya river costs around $10 an hour—or take a private, five-hour tour for around $38. All major hotels arrange excursions.

On both the river and its canals, photo opportunities come thick and fast. Wooden stilt-houses, gilded temples and golden Buddhas, colonial-style mansions, spirit houses, a statue of a Chinese Dragon Lady—all are here. Miniature markets of floating shops row out to tempt you with everything from beer to bananas.

Right on the river, Wat Arun (Temple of the Dawn) takes exoticism to new heights. Below a needle point tower, its walls dazzle with mosaics made of hundreds of thousands of pieces of multi-colored porcelain. Chinese trading ships once used old porcelain as ballasts; here it has been recycled into temple ornamentation.

Visited on most Bangkok tours, another stunning temple is Wat Pho. Inside its 16th-century temple complex, you'll find the mega-sized Reclining Buddha. Thais make offerings of incense, lotus buds, and goldleaf to help keep the Buddha in golden glory. If you want to garner some merit, a small packet of gold leaf costs 40 cents. (As in all Buddhist temples, you must enter the pavilion barefoot.)

In a verdant garden of fishponds, flowers, and spirit houses, Jim

Thompson's House is another Bangkok must-see. Rather than one building, it's actually six traditional Thai houses constructed from teak. It provides a wonderful oasis of tranquillity—and another glimpse of how things used to be.

Elevated on stilts to prevent flooding, the 200-year-old wooden houses were gathered from across central Thailand and re-erected in 1959 on their present site. They're chock-full of antique Buddhas, statuary, and curios. (Look out for the "mouse palace" and the frog- and cat-shaped chamber pots!) The raised wooden boards at each doorway weren't designed to trip up human visitors—they're baffle boards to keep out ghosts and spirits.

An ex-military intelligence agent from Delaware, Jim Thompson is credited with reviving Thailand's hand-woven silk trade. (Hard to believe now, but after World War II, it had dwindled to cottage-industry status.) The story of what happened to Thompson is strange. Born in 1906, an astrologer once warned him to be careful of events during his 61st year. Leaving no clue as to what became of him, Thompson disappeared during a visit to Malaysia's Cameron Highlands in 1967.

To avoid city traffic, the best way to reach Jim Thompson's House (*6 Soi Kasemsan 2, Rama I Road*) is on the Sky-Train—get off at National Stadium Station, and from there it's well sign-posted. Opening hours are 9 a.m. to 5 p.m. Admission is around $2.

Udon Thani

Picture the sun sinking down over the Mekong River, the silhouette of a fisherman trawling for catfish from a long wooden boat. Near the riverside town of Nong Khai, such a view—and an 860-square-foot modern furnished house to go with it—is available through FBI Udon Real Estate for $24,100. The house is 100 yards from the river.

With around 110,000 inhabitants, Udon Thani is as close to a big city as Isaan gets. Vietnam veterans may remember it. The local airport (now with flights to Bangkok and Chiang Mai) is built on the site of a former U.S. air base. From here, bombing raids were launched across into Laos and Vietnam. Udon Thani provided U.S. forces with R&R. Remembering the beauty of the land, some veterans returned, married local girlfriends, and settled here.

The city is a melange of old and modern. Girdled by outdoor food courts (buffet-style meals cost $1.30), In Udon Thani's night market you can find besoms (twig brooms) for sweeping floors, cut flowers, tool-kits, cell-phone accessories, farmers' conical hats for 50 cents, and row upon row of clothing. You'll find arts and crafts that tourists enjoy browsing. This market is for locals—or mostly locals. An elephant swaying down the street carries an advertising sign for the Aussie Pub and Restaurant.

Udon Thani has four nine-hole golf courses. Thirty miles away near Nong Khai, there's also Victory Park, an 18-hole, par 72 course. Prices for a game range from $3.12 to $5.20 in Udon; $13.78 for Victory Park. Expats use the 50-meter pool of Udon's Physical Education College for 78 cents. There are also tennis and badminton facilities, two bowling alleys, and pool and darts in a number of bars. In the cooler evening air, hordes of joggers pound the paths around Nong Prajak Park and Nong Sim Lake.

Udon's City Lodge and Bakery is highly rated amongst expats. (English crumpets are even on the menu.)

Ten minutes walk from the Night Market, Charoensi Shopping Center is northeast Thailand's largest mall: four floors of cell-phone outlets, electronics computers, and photography. You'll even find Kentucky Fried Chicken and Swenson's icecream, and a nine-screen multiplex cinema. The UK pharmacy chain Boots, also has a branch here—and the prices are a lot cheaper than home.

Thai ladies aren't keen on getting a suntan, and skin-whitening products are popular. In Isaan, it's over 90° F every day and many locals carry parasols. Stepping out off the plane at Udon Thani's airport, you're actually offered big black umbrellas as sun protection when crossing the tarmac.

Phuket

Phuket, Thailand's largest island, was hit by the Christmas tsunami—but most residential developments remained unscathed. Almost everything is back to normal now, and a German-designed Early Warning System will be in operation by the time you read this.

Expat contacts tell us it's like nature has cleansed itself, the Andaman Sea is even clearer, and the beaches are lovelier than before. World-famous dive sites are intact. If fact, some large fish that haven't been seen in these waters for decades have returned.

We think Phuket is the nicest coastal option for couples who want to buy or rent in Thailand and live here full-time. Although wonderful for a vacation, Koh Samui is probably too small. And the culture of Pattaya can be depressingly nasty.

Phuket prices? Furnished studio-type condominiums with a communal pool in the Patong area can be found for $39,000 to $50,000. Near Phuket Laguna, you can buy a 1,183-square-foot villa in Thai-Balinese style for $130,000.

High-flying Thai kicks

By Steenie Harvey

What to do on the tropical Thai island of Koh Samui? Well I couldn't resist a few jars of beer and two-and-half hours of full-blooded violence. No, I'm not rampaging around with English soccer thugs...I've got a ringside seat in Chaweng's boxing stadium.

Fights—eight bouts in total—normally take place Tuesdays and Fridays at 9 p.m. This isn't normal boxing, though. This is Muay Thai—traditional Thai kick-boxing. It's vicious: flying feet and fists, as well as elbows and knees crunching into tender parts. Each bout consists of five three-minute rounds. Not all bouts last that long. One poor devil gets kicked in the face and is knocked out stone cold.

Muay Thai is a martial art and much ritual takes place before each fight. Boxers climb into the ring wearing an elaborate headband called a mongkhol. These headbands have been blessed by Buddhist monks: each fighter believes his to be a sacred object bestowing good luck. The contestants then perform a slow dance called the Wai Khru, which essentially pays homage to their teachers. After this is over, the trainers remove the fighters' headbands, and the action starts.

No "Rocky" music here! But there is a band whose instruments are made up of a type of wailing wind pipe, drums, and cymbals. The music accompanies each fight from the start of the homage dance to the final kick or blow.

Thailand starts its fighters off early, often as young as seven. One of tonight's early bouts is between two little guys who both look about 10 years old. I wouldn't dream of getting into an argument with either of them...

The place to see top Muay Thai fighters is Bangkok, but Koh Samui offers a great chance to discover what it's all about. Tickets start at 300 baht ($7.80), but it only costs 800 baht ($20.80) for a ringside seat.

Cost of living

It's hard to put an exact figure on monthly grocery/eating out bills in Thailand. Much depends on your tastes, how often you eat out, and also how much alcohol you drink. (There's some serious drinking done in Udon.)

The following is the monthly breakdown for a three-bedroom apartment in Udon Thani:

- Rent: $245

- Utilities (electricity/water): $27

- Food: $55 (there are lots of small street kitchens, noodle shops etc. that serve nice food costing just 50 to 60 cent per meal)

- Health insurance: $17.13

- Full-time maid service: $73

- Cable TV (61 channels): $6.11

This works out to only $13.91 a day!

A soda is about 50 cents in Thai restaurants, 25 cents in a shop; a beer will set you back only $1 to $1.50 in a restaurant, 50 cents to 60 cents in a shop. A box of cigarettes (Marlboro) costs $1.35; a taxi is just over 70 cents for a three-kilometre (4.8 miles) journey; and gasoline costs 60 cent a liter. There are different types of car insurance, the most expensive (first class insurance) costs between $415 and $513 per year. First year's insurance is included in the price if you buy a new car.

Here's the monthly breakdown for a quality, two-bedroom apartment in the more "touristy"—and, therefore, more expensive—Phuket, that rents for $1,020 monthly:

- Common charges for residence with pool, security: $128

- Utilities including air conditioning: $81

- Expanded cable TV package: $40

- Landline phone for Internet/local calls: $15

- Maid service: $100

- Eating out in a mid-priced restaurant, three times a week (for a couple): $35

- Other food/household goods (estimated): $500

This comes to $30 a day for a couple.

The Retirement Visa

For the Retirement Visa, or "O" Visa, in Thailand, the requirements are straightforward. The applicant must be 50 years old or more at the time of application, and cannot work in Thailand. The would-be retiree must demonstrate that he or she has at least $20,000 in the bank, an income of $1,625 per month, or a combination that would add up to $20,000 each year. There are other requirements to extend this visa that mostly involve having a set amount of money in Thailand.

Other types of visa

The Tourist Visa: Citizens of most developed western countries as well as wealthy Asian countries can automatically be issued a visa at the border or the airport, after displaying a valid passport. This is known as a Tourist Visa and is usually issued for a 30-day period. Should you apply in advance of your arrival, you may be granted a 60-day Tourist Visa. Tourist Visas can be extended for 10 days at a time, but the fee for this recently increased to discourage foreigners from living in Thailand indefinitely on this visa. Many people have lived in Thailand for years on Tourist Visas by simply leaving the country and returning every 30 days. Singapore, Malaysia, Burma, Cambodia, Laos, Vietnam, and the Philippines are all "visa-run" favorites.

The Non-Immigrant Visa: For those who wish to stay longer in Thailand, you have two options: A Non-Immigrant Visa is issued for 90 days for a variety of reasons, but most commonly for business purposes and to a lesser extent, for spouses of Thai nationals. The Non-Immigrant "B" Visa for business may be issued to foreigners who work in Thailand and, in many cases, for investors. A considerable pile of paperwork is involved, but there are many reputable legal firms that can get your package arranged for a reasonable fee. The most important ingredient for applying is a verified employment contract with a company licensed to do business in Thailand. Many expats choose to form Thai companies and hire themselves. Naturally, this is also a complicated process that requires legal guidance.

After the Non Immigrant "B" is issued, applicants are generally issued a 90-day, single-entry visa. This gets the applicant back into Thailand, free, and allows him or her to stay for 90 days. If the individual needs to leave Thailand before 90 days are up, he or she must report to a local immigration office, and receive another entry permit. This visa can be renewed for 90 days at a time. If the foreigner is granted a work permit (yet another paper maze), he or she can be granted a multi-entry visa for one year. In this way, the individual can leave the country without applying for another entry, and only needs to report to the immigration office every 90 days. This type of visa can also be extended and renewed.

There are other types of visas for Thailand, but they are mostly for very specialized situations or are practically unattainable. For information, go to the Ministry of Foreign Affairs' website at: *www.mfa.go.th/web*.

Two years on in Thailand
By John Seely

We'd been regular visitors to Thailand for years so, when we finally decided to make a permanent home here, we had an idea what we were letting ourselves in for. The low cost, and the high standard of living attracted us, as did the warm welcome extended to foreigners. We decided on the mountainous northern section of the country, because it offered the best climate for us, and was unspoiled and undeveloped. At the same time, it had all the modern conveniences we needed and was easy to get to. So, three years ago, for $13,000, we made an offer on 20 acres of a quiet corner of a mountain, three miles outside the regional capital, Chiang Rai. It was what we had always dreamed of. Surrounded by hills and farms with not another house in sight—and within minutes of a modern shopping center, good medical facilities and an international airport—it seemed perfect. We couldn't wait until it was ours.

The first obstacle

Whoa. Not so fast. Buying land in Thailand is very complicated. There are five levels of ownership, and to make things more difficult, non-Thais cannot own land at all. We had to use a proxy. The land we bought didn't belong to anyone 30 years ago. As the area opened up and became more accessible, people moved in. They claimed land for farms and villages, and registered their claims. This gave them the right to live on and use the land, but not to transfer ownership. Even if the land was sold, it was still registered in the original name. We looked at several plots where no proof could be offered that the person selling was in fact the owner, and so steered well clear. Many people, Thais as well as foreigners, have bought land only to find out later that someone else also has claimed ownership.

When we bought, we had a list of previous owners, their sale contracts, and the original registration papers. We also had our deal witnessed by attorneys. We visited the forestry department to check that it wasn't restricted land, and also visited the village head man to verify that the person selling really was the owner. Our area is now being upgraded, and we've been told that in another year or so we will have clear title. This is doubly good news, not only because we will have the extra security of title, but also because the value of our land will rise as it can then be used as collateral with a bank.

Previously, our farm was used to grow dry rice and corn. Nobody lived there. It wasn't even fenced, the boundary being marked by clumps of bananas and bamboo. There were no amenities, and the road was a dusty track. The road is still dirt, but everything else has changed.

We dug a deep well, installed a pump and tanks, brought in electricity from a mile away, and had telephones installed. We planted trees, built a house, and then wondered if we'd not made a terrible mistake.

Giant lizards and cobras

Friends advised us to do something with the land immediately to show that we were planning to use it, as the government was prosecuting speculators sitting on unimproved property. We decided to build a simple bungalow that we could easily rebuild if we wanted. I was working in Taiwan then, so we couldn't spend a lot of time with builders and architects. In fact, we copied the locals and did without an architect altogether. We said: "We want a house so big with so many rooms." The builders then turned up one day and said: "Right, we'll start here."

For $6,000 we got a three-bedroom bungalow with a paper-thin roof that is unbearably hot in the summer. We also have termites chewing at every doorpost, because the foundation is too thin. Giant lizards slip through the gap between the walls and the ceiling, and cobras get in the kitchen. But it is functional, and we spend most of the day outside anyway. If we'd been less rushed, we would have oriented the house to avoid the afternoon sun while catching the cool night breezes from the mountains. At present, we have the opposite.

Enough is enough

This year, we decided enough was enough and are now in the middle of replacing the roof and installing insulation. We're having an extension built as well, in case we want to start a farm-stay B&B. Again, we did not employ an architect, reckoning we could plan it ourselves—a big mistake, as misunderstandings have been numerous. What was going to be a three-month project is now well into its fifth month, and is still only half done.

Everything is possible here, but a great deal of patience and perseverance is needed to get what you want, the way you want it. We hardly dare leave the site, even for a morning, because we fear something will go wrong if we do.

A plus to living here is the lack of planning restrictions. We bought a hill, and built a house, and planted an orchard on it. We didn't have to get planning permission, and could have built a castle had we wished. Of course, there's nothing to stop someone building a piggery or outdoor karaoke bar next-door, either.

We have planted more than 700 lychee and mango trees, among others, as the start of a farm. We have high hopes that in another two years or so we will have enough fruit to start selling commercially and, who knows, we may even make a profit one of these years. We would think twice about buying so much land in the future, though.

Not because we know as much about farming as we do about building space rockets—looking out over the rows of healthy trees gives me great pleasure—but because of the difficulty we've experienced in getting reliable labor, as well as the sheer amount of work that has been involved.

A three-day funeral

We would hire laborers, and for a few days all would be well. Then they wouldn't turn up because it rained too hard during the night, or because someone had a birthday, or because the second cousin of their mother's best friend had died and they had to go to the funeral for three days. There is a casual approach to work here, and it takes getting used to. Meanwhile, the trees need care, and the grass is overgrown.

We spend most of our time pottering on the farm, which is what we wanted. We didn't come here to sit on the balcony swooshing flies all day, but we also didn't want to be tied down 9-to-5. The low cost of living means we can live well on the rent we get from our house in England. The farm provides us with plenty to do, and the prospect of a good income in the years ahead, as well as a place to spend our retirement. And we can take off whenever we want, when we're not building. When we need a change, we take off to Bangkok, or Singapore, or one of Thailand's unspoiled islands or beaches.

We have full-time, live-in help for just $120 a month. Aaw helps in the house, and with our animals, while her husband, Oowun, does most of the farm work. If we go away, we leave them in charge.

Patience is a virtue

Since we've been here, we've had no really bad experiences, though there have been plenty of petty annoyances. Thailand is a developing country, so we can't expect the same standards that we would in the West. I sometimes forget this, and get myself needlessly worked up. Still, most of our experiences have been positive, and we feel comfortable here.

It would have been simpler to buy an existing property with utilities already installed, rather than starting from scratch. Although we had visited the area many times at different seasons, we should have followed the advice of *International Living* and rented for a year before we bought.

This would have given us a better idea of the pros and cons of different areas. We were shocked by the noise from river traffic during some seasons, for example, even though it is a mile away.

Noisy all-night fairs are held nearby, and we have found that April, as well as being very, very hot, is also unbearably smoggy because of the fires lit by farmers clearing their fields. Entire hillsides can be in flames, and the air gets thick with smoke and cinders.

I've never felt any resentment from the locals about my being "one of those damn foreigners, coming in and buying up our land." Nearly everyone living here is from somewhere else. My neighbors include an American, an Italian, and a Frenchman. Another is from Pakistan. Down the road is a hostel funded by a Japanese charity. Nearby, an extended Yunnanese family lives next to immigrants from Laos and the south of Thailand. Hill tribesmen from Burma make up the bulk of the local village. With this sort of ethnic mixture, why should I feel an outsider? It's not as if everyone can even speak Thai well, which makes me feel a lot better about my feeble attempts at the language.

Contacts

Real estate

- **Udon Real Estate** (Mr. Preben Pretzmann), *411/38 Hlang Pramong Road, Tambon Hmarkkhaeng, Amphur Muang Udon Thani, Udon Thani 41000, Thailand; tel. (66)42-24-63 78; cell (66)72-229-826; email: fbi@udonrealestate.com.*

- **Fair Properties** (Malai Buraphin or J.R. Belgraver), *340/11 View Talay Condo, Building B, Tappraya Road, Pattaya, Chonburi 20260, Thailand; tel. (66)383-03-177; e-mail: fairproperties@hotmail.com; website: www.fairproperties.com.*

- **Skandinavian Super Houses**, *315/175, 176 Moo. 12, Thappraya Road, Jomtien, Thailand; tel. (66)38-303-766; e-mail: mail@thaisuperhouse.com.*

- **Asia Properties Group** (David Mitchell), *178/1 Sukhumvit Road, Bangkok 10110, Thailand; tel. (66)2-252-6290; e-mail: dwmitchell@asia-properties.net; website: www.asia-properties.net.*

Embassies

- **American Citizen Services (ACS)**, *95 Wireless Road, Bangkok 10330, Thailand; tel. (66)2205-4049; email: acsbkk@state.gov; website: http://bangkok.usembassy.gov/ embassy/acs.*

- **Royal Thai Embassy**, *1024 Wisconsin Avenue, N.W., Suite 401, Washington, D.C. 20007; tel. (202)944-3600; fax (202)944-3611; website: www.thaiembdc.org; email: thai.wsn@thaiembdc.org.*

Private Health Insurance for Expats

One of the most frequently asked questions we receive at *International Living* has to do with medical insurance for Americans abroad. As you probably realize, your U.S. health insurance usually does not travel beyond U.S. borders. Some providers in some countries will accept Blue Cross and other American insurance providers—but don't count on it.

It's worth taking a look at the Allnation Insurance Company. It provides health insurance to expatriates worldwide under the age of 65. You can buy a "Classic Gold" policy or a "Select Silver" (more modest) one. To give you an idea of fees and coverage:

Typically, Allnation pays 80% of the first $5,000 of covered allowable charges and then pays for covered services at 100%. A healthy 55-year-old male, for example, with a "Select Silver" policy in Region 3 (Argentina, Bolivia, Chile, Paraguay, Uruguay, Western Europe, Africa), with a $1,000 deductible, would pay about $3,108 in annual premiums.

- **Allnation Insurance Company**, *1201 N. Orange Street, Suite 716 Floor, Wilmington, DE 19801-1186; tel. in the U.S. (800)342-0719; website: www.allnation.com.*

Another Insurance company worth looking at is PHA Expat. Established in 1995, PHA Expat is a specialist in health care intermediaries, dealing with over 30 insurance agencies. The premiums PHA quote are exactly the same as you can obtain directly, but in some cases they can offer preferential rates, and "cash back" offers such as a 5% discount on renewal of premiums.

PHA Expat will allow you to take out annual health insurance premiums giving cover solely for Europe. However, as with most European companies, the maximum age for eligibility is 64 years.

We don't have space to list all the various PHA health plans, levels of cover, and benefits. However, the "Comprehensive Plan"—which would be more than sufficient for most people—offers approximately $1.8 million cover (Europe only). Annual rates start at $964 for those up to age 25. For those in the 60-to-64 age group, the annual premiums are $ 3,831. If you're already a member before you reach the age of 65, you're still eligible up to the age of 75. The premium for 70- to 74-year-olds is $9,246. You can find all of PHA Expat rates on its informative website.

- **PHA Expat**, *89 Station Road, Sidcup, Kent DA15 7DN, United Kingdom; tel. (44)870-770-0946; fax (44)208-309-2909; e-mail: expat@phauk.com; website: www.phaexpat.com.*

BUPA International is another major name in expat health insurance. BUPA's international coverage rates for U.S. citizens (under the Essential, Classic, and Gold schemes) are listed below, and correct as of the time of going to print.

Rates vary depending on the country where you plan to spend the majority of the year. The rates on the next page apply to the following coutries: Bahamas, Beliz, Bermuda, Bolivia, Cayman Islands, Chile, Colombia, Costa Rica, Greece, Haiti, Honduras, Israel, Jamaica, Mexico, Nicaragua, Panama, Paraguay, Turkey, and Uruguay. For rates on other countries, visit Bupa International's website (see below).

- Essential: In-patient treatment up to $900,000

- Classic: In-patient, out-patient treatment and routine maternity cover up to $1,200,000

- Gold: In-patient, out-patient treatment and routine maternity cover and emergency dental cover up to $1,600,000

- **BUPA International**, *Russell Mews, Brighton BN1 2NR, United Kingdom; tel. (44)1273-208-181; fax (44)1273-866-583; website: www.bupa-intl.com.*

Age	Lifeline Essential Scheme	Lifeline Classic Scheme	Lifeline Gold Scheme
0 to 19	681 – 792	938 – 1,104	1,179 – 1,394
20 to 24	845 – 1,098	1,185 – 1,545	1,496 – 1,925
25 to 29	1,156 – 1,327	1,624 – 1,827	2,007 – 2,265
30 to 34	1,352 – 1,446	1,853 – 1,988	2,310 – 2,477
35 to 39	1,467 – 1,613	2,027 – 2,225	2,515 – 2,740
40 to 44	1,662 – 1,878	2,283 – 2,571	2,816 – 3,123
45 to 49	1,937 – 2,168	2,657 – 2,972	3,203 – 3,575
50 to 54	2,225 – 2,600	3,046 – 3,464	3,680 – 4,234
55 to 59	2,727 – 3,334	3,599 – 4,337	4,407 – 5,442
60 to 64	3,510 – 4,565	4,572 – 5,996	5,784 – 7,530
65 to 69	4,916 – 6,021	6,471 – 7,985	8,064 – 9,823
70 to 74	6,221 – 7,049	8,266 – 9,323	10,169 – 11,819
75 to 79	7,265 – 8,145	9,571 – 10,710	12,298 – 13,891
80 to 120	8,369 – 8,817	11,033 – 11,675	14,208 – 14,840

International Living's 2005 Global Retirement Index

⟨ᐁᐁ⟩

For the fifth year in a row, Panama has taken top honors in our Annual Global Retirement Index. It comes out on top in every category, including the Special Benefits (for retirees) category, by boasting the world's best *pensionado* program, which is far superior to the famed Costa Rica program of the 1980s. Plus it boasts a low cost of living, affordable real estate, and great weather in the interior. Also, it has something extraordinary and unique for this part of the world— Panama City, a First-World city with infrastructure that works, U.S.-style shopping malls, nightclubs, restaurants, and cafés.

How our Global Retirement Index is scored

- **Real estate**. Countries with low real estate prices, and where purchasing real estate is relatively easy, receive the highest scores. We use our own experiences, plus reports from our contributing editors and real estate contacts around the world, to rate each country. Weight: 15%

- **Entertainment, Recreation, and Culture**. This category considers the number of newspapers per 1,000 citizens, the number of museums and cinemas per capita, the number of university students, the literacy rate, and the variety of cultural and recreational offerings. Weight: 10%

- **Cost of living**. This score is based on statistics from the Indexes of Living Costs Abroad, Quarter Allowances, and Hardship Differentials, published by the U.S. Department of State, and on data published by Business International. We also use our first-hand experiences living and traveling in

Country	Real Estate	Special Benefits	Cost of Living	Culture
Panama	80	100	80	62
France	75	63	62	93
Malta	65	65	74	77
Mexico	82	60	80	65
Romania	89	65	83	71
Italy	58	64	73	85
Cyprus	80	76	60	72
Nicaragua	85	68	80	53
Uruguay	85	35	85	64
New Zealand	65	40	65	77
Belize	45	88	77	60
Spain	68	49	76	69
Chile	70	47	75	65
Argentina	75	29	80	71
Slovenia	75	46	63	76
Ecuador	87	31	83	55
Portugal	62	23	77	71
Malaysia	85	55	73	71
Poland	81	23	63	72
Greece	68	49	60	67
U.K.	10	55	58	89
South Africa	81	23	69	60
Thailand	90	10	80	69
Dominican Rep.	45	55	80	49
Ireland	10	79	55	72
Croatia	65	10	60	61
Honduras	65	19	80	50
U.S.	10	7	74	84

these countries. The lower the score, the higher the cost of living. Weight: 20%

- **Safety and stability**. This measure of social unrest in each country is based primarily on Interpol data and State Department statistics. It also takes into account the civil liberties and political rights granted by each government. Our own experiences and reports from expatriates living in these countries also influence the safety scores. Weight: 5%

Health	Infrastructure	Safety/ Stability	Climate	Total
73	60	100	74	81
100	99	100	80	80
95	64	100	100	78
80	66	92	98	76
70	57	80	72	75
80	65	100	74	73
70	60	100	70	72
65	45	80	75	71
75	58	100	87	70
92	77	100	72	69
70	40	70	58	68
70	59	100	76	68
77	50	100	62	67
74	53	100	90	67
74	56	100	75	67
74	43	70	100	67
89	58	100	90	67
65	25	80	40	66
82	53	80	67	63
70	50	70	75	62
90	64	100	60	62
70	57	90	78	62
71	48	72	54	61
67	56	70	57	61
69	60	100	60	60
81	56	100	91	58
67	43	70	81	58
65	100	100	91	54

- **Health care**. Considered in this category are the cost of a typical visit to a general practitioner, and the cost and coverage particulars of health insurance. Weight: 20%

- **Climate**. Countries with temperate weather throughout the year, moderate rainfall, and little risk of natural disaster, come out on top in this category. We use data representing each country as a whole, instead of favoring one region over another. Weight: 5%

- **Special benefits**. This category considers government provisions that make moving to, and living in each country easier and more affordable for foreigners. Taken into account are property rights for foreign residents, property tax rates, duty-free imports on personal belongings, currency controls, employment restrictions, voting rights, and transportation discounts for seniors. Weight: 20%

- **Infrastructure**. This section considers the number of cars and telephones per 1,000 residents, the length of railroad track in usable condition, the number of airports, the quality of the country's road and highway network, and the availability of telecommunications. Weight: 5%